LANGUAGE IN USE

PRE-INTERMEDIATE

CLASSROOM BOOK

Adrian Doff
Christopher Jones

CAMBRIDGE
UNIVERSITY PRESS

Published by the Press Syndicate of the University of Cambridge
The Pitt Building, Trumpington Street, Cambridge CB2 1RP
40 West 20th Street, New York, NY 10011–4211, USA
10 Stamford Road, Oakleigh, Melbourne 3166, Australia

First published 1991
Fifth printing 1995

Printed in Great Britain at the University Press, Cambridge

ISBN 0 521 37851 6   Classroom Book
ISBN 0 521 37852 4   Self-study Workbook
ISBN 0 521 40602 1   Self-study Workbook with Answer Key
ISBN 0 521 37853 2   Teacher's Book
ISBN 0 521 37248 8   Class Cassette Set
ISBN 0 521 37247 X   Self-study Cassette Set

Split editions:
ISBN 0 521 40835 0   Classroom Book A
ISBN 0 521 40836 9   Classroom Book B
ISBN 0 521 40837 7   Self-study Workbook A with Answer Key
ISBN 0 521 40838 5   Self-study Workbook B with Answer Key
ISBN 0 521 40839 3   Self-study Cassette A
ISBN 0 521 40840 7   Self-study Cassette B

Authors' acknowledgements

A large number of people have contributed to *Language in Use*. We would especially like to thank the following:

– for contributing to the listening material: Maria Bardolini, Carolyn Becket, Jan-Bert van den Berg, Catherine Boyce, Frederico Campomori, Bryan Cruden, Peter Davison, Brigitte Dold, Stella Forge, Ines García, Cathy Hall, Josephine Jones, Mary Ann Julian, Muhammad Munasser, Louisa Preskett, Patrick Rayner, Dr Lawrie Reznek, Diana Seavill, Ewa Simbieda, Martin Stolle, Angelice Tagliaferri, Djasminar Tasman, Kumiko Thomas, Francesca Walpot, Carsten Williams, Larissa Williams; and all the actors whose voices were recorded in studio sessions.
– for contributing to the reading material: Michael Carrier, Brigitte Dold, Val Grove, Josephine Jones, Larissa Williams, Tony Williams and Douglas Young.
– for advice and feedback on the Pilot material: Norman Coe, Diane Gruber, Claire MacGregor, Pam Murphy, Alison Piper, Diane Phillips, Stuart Redman, Norman Whitney; and the many teachers and institutions who used the Pilot material in class.
– Peter and Marie-Madeleine Brandt for the cottage in Marathia, and Alastair and Susan Cowan for Eastside Farm.
– Bryan Cruden, Nan Mulder and Larissa Williams for contributing artwork to the Pilot edition.
– Beverly Holmström, Bob Kirby and Bryan Cruden of Edinburgh Language Foundation for their help in organising recordings.
– Carolyn Becket for help in making and editing recordings.
– Hazel Jones for continuous advice and support.

– Peter Taylor of Taylor Riley Productions Ltd, and Peter Thompson and Diana Thompson of Studio AVP, for organising and conducting recording sessions, and for producing the final tapes.
– Peter Ducker MSTD for his work on the Pilot edition.
– Sandie Huskinson-Rolfe of Photoseekers for photo research.
– Ken Brooks for work on text.
– Alison Silver for editing the Self-study Workbook.

We would also like to thank all those at Cambridge University Press who have been involved in the development of the course:
– Adrian du Plessis for his help in initiating the project.
– Colin Hayes for his continuing support and help.
– Peter Donovan for organising and steering the project through its various stages.
– Nick Newton and Joanne Currie for designing the course.
– Alison Baxter, Lindsay White and Nicholas Otway for their work on the Pilot edition.
– Sue Featherstone and Val Grove for general administrative help.
– Cathy Hall, our Desk Editor, for her thoroughness, professionalism and good judgement, and also for her many valuable and constructive contributions to the final version of *Language in Use*.

Contents

Guide to units

Classroom Book

Self-study Workbook

1 Description

Saying what there is and where things are; describing features

Grammar: There is/are; have/has got; place prepositions

Grammar exercises
Listening: *Asking for help*
Pronunciation: *Where's the stress?*
Reading: *Islands*

2 Family and friends

Vocabulary: family; relationships; love and marriage

Reading and listening activity: *Are you a loner?*

Vocabulary exercises
Listening: *Relatives*
Sound and spelling: *Words with* a
Writing skills: *Sentences*

3 Habits, customs and facts

Talking about repeated activities and things that are generally true

Grammar: Present simple tense; frequency expressions

Grammar exercises
Listening: *Japanese New Year*
Pronunciation: *The sound /ə/*
Reading: *Reptiles and amphibians*

4 Going places

Vocabulary: vehicles; public transport; talking about travel

Reading and listening activity: *Airport*

Vocabulary exercises
Listening: *Likes and dislikes*
Sound and spelling: *Words with* e
Writing skills: *Punctuation*

5 Now

Talking about things happening 'now' and 'around now'; describing scenes

Grammar: Present continuous tense; There is/are + -ing

Grammar exercises
Listening: *These days*
Pronunciation: *Reduced vowels (1)*
Reading: *What's going on?*

6 Food and drink

Vocabulary: food and drink; meals; restaurants

Reading and listening activity: *Cholesterol and your heart*

Vocabulary exercises
Listening: *Polish dishes*
Sound and spelling: *Words with* i
Writing skills: *Reference*

Revision and extension Units 1–6

Classroom Book	Self-study Workbook

7 The past

Talking about past events; saying when things happened; telling stories

Grammar: Past simple tense; time expressions

Grammar exercises
Listening: *When did you last ... ?*
Pronunciation: *Reduced vowels (2)*
Reading: *Jokes*

8 Somewhere to live

Vocabulary: houses and flats; rooms and furniture

Reading and listening activity: *Haunted houses*

Vocabulary exercises
Listening: *Favourite rooms*
Sound and spelling: *Words with* o *(1)*
Writing skills: *Joining ideas*

9 Quantity

Talking about quantity; saying there is too much and not enough

Grammar: a/some/any; quantity expressions; How much/many ... ?; too & not enough

Grammar exercises
Listening: *Panel discussion*
Pronunciation: *Secondary stress*
Reading: *Money*

10 Clothes

Vocabulary: items of clothing; materials and patterns; buying and wearing clothes

Reading and listening activity: *Going for gold*

Vocabulary exercises
Listening: *Working clothes*
Sound and spelling: *Words with* o *(2)*
Writing skills: *Sequence (1)*

11 Future plans

Talking about intentions and plans; talking about future arrangements

Grammar: going to; Present continuous tense; will; future time expressions

Grammar exercises
Listening: *Two journeys*
Pronunciation: *Rhythm*
Reading: *Letters*

12 How do you feel?

Vocabulary: aches and pains; remedies; going to the doctor

Reading and listening activity: *All in the mind*

Vocabulary exercises
Listening: *Feeling ill*
Sound and spelling: *Words with* u
Writing skills: *Listing*

Revision and extension Units 7–12

Classroom Book	Self-study Workbook

13 Comparison

Making comparisons; expressing
preferences; describing outstanding features

Grammar: comparative adjectives; than;
superlative adjectives

Grammar exercises
Listening: *The most and the least*
Pronunciation: *Reduced vowels (3)*
Reading: *Four planets*

14 About town

Vocabulary: amenities; giving directions;
describing towns in general

Reading and listening activity: *Los Angeles*

Vocabulary exercises
Listening: *Living in London*
Sound and spelling: *Words with* y
Writing skills: *Reason and contrast*

15 Past and present

Talking about changes; announcing news;
talking about experiences

Grammar: Present perfect tense; still;
not ... yet; Have you ever ... ?

Grammar exercises
Listening: *Have you ever ... ?*
Pronunciation: *Falling intonation*
Reading: *Varieties of English*

16 Free time

Vocabulary: leisure activities; sports; likes and
dislikes

Reading and listening activity: *Board games
round the world*

Vocabulary exercises
Listening: *Rock climbing*
Sound and spelling: *Words with* r
Writing skills: *Sequence (2)*

17 Obligation

Giving rules; talking about obligation; giving
advice

Grammar: must(n't); (don't) have to; can('t);
should(n't); ought (not) to

Grammar exercises
Listening: *Radio phone-in*
Pronunciation: *Rising intonation*
Reading: *Rules of the game*

18 A day's work

Vocabulary: names of jobs; talking about
work; careers

Reading and listening activity: *Applying for a
job*

Vocabulary exercises
Listening: *A security guard*
Sound and spelling: *Hard and soft* c *and* g
Writing skills: *Letter writing*

Revision and extension Units 13–18

Guide to units

Classroom Book

Self-study Workbook

19 Narration

Talking about past events and their circumstances; telling stories

Grammar: Past continuous tense; Past simple tense; when & while

Grammar exercises
Listening: *Two stories*
Pronunciation: *Intonation: questions*
Reading: *Bad luck*

20 People

Vocabulary: physical appearance; age; personal characteristics

Reading and listening activity: *The Dream Game*

Vocabulary exercises
Listening: *Famous people*
Sound and spelling: *Long and short vowels*
Writing skills: *Relative clauses (1)*

21 Prediction

Making predictions; talking about consequences

Grammar: will, won't & might; if/unless + Present simple; going to

Grammar exercises
Listening: *Driving test*
Pronunciation: *Contrastive stress*
Reading: *Star gazing*

22 Around the world

Vocabulary: geographical features; weather and climate; countries and nationalities

Reading and listening activity: *Car chaos*

Vocabulary exercises
Listening: *Living in a hot climate*
Sound and spelling: *Words with* s
Writing skills: *Relative clauses (2)*

23 Duration

Talking about activities that are still going on; asking and talking about duration

Grammar: Present perfect continuous and simple; How long ...?; for & since; spend (+ -ing)

Grammar exercises
Listening: *24 hours*
Pronunciation: *Dialogues*
Reading: *General knowledge quiz*

24 But is it art?

Vocabulary: art and literature; writers, artists and performers

Reading and listening activity: *The Night in the Hotel*

Vocabulary exercises
Listening: *Choosing a painting*
Sound and spelling: *Words with* th
Writing skills: *Sequence (3)*

Revision and extension Units 19–24

1 Description

1 Behind the door

There is/are • has got

1 Look at the first door and imagine the room behind it. Examples:

There's a map on the wall.
There are some desks.
It's got a blackboard.
It's got white walls.

2 Write sentences about one of the other rooms. Use words from the box, and add ideas of your own.

bed	table	telephone
chair	magazine	reception desk
lift	shower	television
menu	computer	'no smoking' sign

Show your sentences to another student.

2 Good points and bad points

Negative forms

1 Look at these three letters, and complete the last sentence in each one.

A It hasn't got a language lab, but there's a video and there are cassette players in all the classrooms. The building's quite small, so there isn't a

B It's a beautiful place, and it's got some lovely beaches. Unfortunately, it's a bit quiet in the evenings. There aren't any

C I have to share my room with two other people, and there's only one bathroom on each floor. The worst thing is, it hasn't got

2 Continue these remarks.

    a It isn't a very interesting town to live in.
    b They live in a really unusual house.
    c I have to work in this terrible little office.
    d It's an incredibly small island.
    e It's not a very good library.

3 Hotel

Questions

1 You're thinking of staying at this hotel, and you want to find out about it. Write down some questions.

> Is there a … ?
>
> Are there any … ?
>
> Has the hotel got … ?
>
> Have the rooms got … ?

2 🔲 You will hear three people talking about the hotel.

    a Which of your questions do they answer?
    b Is this a good hotel for
      – a group of students?
      – someone on a business trip?
      – a retired couple?

4 Where are they?

Place prepositions

next to	in front of	opposite
near	behind	between
in	above	below

1 **Find places in the pictures where you can:**

   a post a letter
   b make a phone call
   c buy a newspaper
   d have a snack
   e go to the toilet
   f change some money
   g buy a plane ticket

Where are they? Use words from the box.

2 **Ask and answer questions.**

> Excuse me. Is there a post box near here?

> Yes. There's one opposite the cinema.

3 **Find out about places in the town where you are now.**

Grammar Checklist

There is/are

There is + *singular nouns*
There are + *plural nouns*

There's a bank near the station.
There are some shops near the station.
   (*not* ~~There's some shops~~ ...)

Negatives: **There isn't / There aren't**

There isn't an airport here.
There aren't any buses today.

Questions: **Is there?/Are there?**

There's a bank → **Is there** a bank?
There are some shops → **Are there** any shops?

'one'

Is there a post box near here?
There's **one** at the corner. (= ... a post box ...)

have/has got

I/you/we/they + **'ve got** (= have got)
He/she/it + **'s got** (= has got)

All the classrooms **have got** TV.
The school**'s got** a library.

Negatives: **haven't got / hasn't got**

They **haven't got** any children.
The hotel **hasn't got** a swimming pool.

Questions: **Have/Has** + *subject* + **got**

Have they **got** any children?
Has the school **got** a library?

See also Reference section, page 130.

Focus on Form

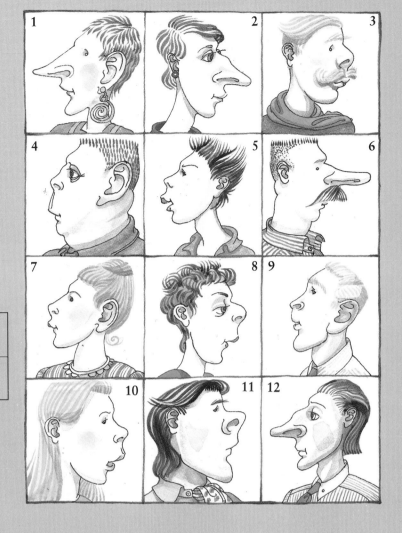

1 There is/are

Work in pairs. Look at the picture on page 115.

Student A: Look at the picture for 20 seconds. Then close your book, and try to remember what there is in the picture. Examples:

> *There's a* bottle.
> *There are some* matches.

Student B: Check A's answers.

There's another picture on page 117.

2 There is/are: questions

Ask questions with
Is there a(n) …? or
Are there any …?

Answer from the table.

Examples:

Yes		is.
	there	are.
No		isn't.
		aren't.

cities in Antarctica?
A Are there any cities in Antarctica?
B No, there aren't.

opera house in Sydney?
A Is there an opera house in Sydney?
B Yes, there is.

a opera house in your town?
b lakes in Saudi Arabia?
c American flag on the Moon?
d volcanoes in Japan?
e elephants in India?
f metro in Tokyo?
g people on Mars?
h monster in Loch Ness?

3 Have(n't) got & has(n't) got

Student A: Write six sentences about yourself and your house or flat, using *have(n't) got* and *has(n't) got*. Make some true and some false. Examples:

I've got three children.
I haven't got a car.
My bedroom's got orange walls.
My house hasn't got a garden.

Student B: Guess which sentences are true, and which are false.

4 Has got: questions

Student A: Choose one of the pictures above.

Student B: Find out which picture A has chosen. Ask questions with *Has he/she got …?*

Examples: B Has he got dark hair?
            A Yes, he has.
            B Has he got a moustache?
            A No, he hasn't.

5 Pronunciation

How do you say the words and phrases below?

a There's a café on the top floor.
   There are some beautiful beaches.

b Is there a post box near here?
   Are there any toilets?

c The office has got two phones.
   The hotel's got a swimming pool.

d There aren't any good restaurants.
   There isn't a telephone.
   He hasn't got a beard.

🔲 Now listen and check your answers.

2 Family and friends

1 Photo album

1 These are photos of a young woman's family and friends.
Which do you think shows

  – herself?   – her flat-mate?
  – her older brother?   – her parents?
  – her younger brother?   – her brother's girlfriend?
  – her boyfriend?   – her next-door neighbours?
  – her grandmother?

 Listen to the tape.
Which photos does the woman describe?

2 Imagine that this photo shows three of your
family or friends (or use a real photo). Tell
your partner who is in the photo, and say a
few things about each of them.

2 In the family

1 Do you come from a large family? Write numbers in the table, and compare your table with your partner's.

2 Talk about members of your family. Choose any of the questions, and say a few things about the person.

Who's …
… the oldest?   … the youngest?
… the richest?   … the poorest?
… the nicest?   … the most interesting?

How many have you got?	
grandparents	
aunts and uncles	
cousins	
brothers and sisters	
nieces and nephews	
grandchildren	

3 Love story

They fly off to the Caribbean for their honeymoon.

She takes him home to meet her parents, and he does the same.

They get married, and invite all their friends and relations to the wedding.

John and Mary meet at a party. A friend introduces them.

They start going out together regularly.

They decide to get engaged, and he buys her a diamond ring.

They move into a small flat together.

They have a baby daughter, and they call her Anna, after Mary's mother.

He invites her out to see a film, and afterwards they have dinner together.

1 **Work in pairs. Put the story in the most likely order.**

2 **Do you like the story as it is? Make up your own version. Change it in any way you like.**

4 Are you a loner?

READING

Are you a loner?

Do you like other people?

Or do you prefer your own company?

Answer the questions, and find out …

1 Where do you think is the best place to live?

   a in the town centre
   b in a suburb
   c in the country, but quite near a town
   d right out in the country

2 It's your birthday. Do you:

   a have a big party?
   b meet a few friends for a drink?
   c go out for a meal with a close friend?
   d go to bed with a good book?

3 Which kind of holiday would you enjoy the most?

   a staying at a busy seaside town with lots to do in the evenings
   b driving and camping with a group of friends
   c a quiet stay in the country with your family
   d going off alone on a walking holiday

4 A friend invites you to a party. You go, and find you don't know any of the other guests. Do you:

   a make lots of new friends?
   b ask your friend to introduce you to a few people?
   c stay close to your friend?
   d sit in a corner quite happily?

5 You're alone on New Year's Eve. How do you feel?

   a very lonely
   b a bit lonely
   c you don't really mind
   d pleased

6 Would you enjoy any of these? Tick (✔) the boxes.

   ☐ eating in a restaurant alone
   ☐ going on a long journey alone
   ☐ going swimming alone
   ☐ going to the cinema alone
   ☐ spending a weekend alone at home
   ☐ cooking a big meal just for yourself

See your score opposite ⇨

LISTENING

📼 You will hear someone answering the questions in the quiz.

1 Listen, and note down his answers. Then work out his score. Is he a loner?

2 Listen to his answer to question 5 again, and put the pictures in the right order.

Question	Answers				Score
1	a	b	c	d	
2	a	b	c	d	
3	a	b	c	d	
4	a	b	c	d	
5	a	b	c	d	
6					
	Total score:				

A

B

C

D

E

KEY

Scoring
Questions 1–5: a = 1; b = 3; c = 5; d = 7
Question 6: 1 for each tick (✓)

Type A (5–13 points)
You certainly like being with other people, don't you? Do you spend any time alone? Other people are a lot of fun – but remember that being alone can be fun too. Try it some time!

Type B (14–23 points)
You have a busy social life. You like other people, but you also like to keep a little time for yourself. Be careful not to do too much – keep some evenings free to sit and relax quietly at home.

Type C (24–33 points)
You're rather quiet. You like being alone, but you're happiest with a close friend or relation. Big parties are definitely not for you. Your motto is 'Two's company – three's a crowd'.

Type D (34–41 points)
You're a real loner – you would probably be quite happy living on a desert island. But don't forget that there are a lot of other people in the world – and some of them are as interesting as you are!

---

3 Habits, customs and facts

1 Lifestyles

Present simple tense • Yes/no questions

1 [cassette] You will hear part of an interview with a woman called Margarita, who works in a café by the beach.

a Listen and complete the table.

	Summer	Winter
Margarita	works in a café	
Her parents		
Her brother		

b Complete these sentences:
In the winter, they don't …
Margarita's brother doesn't …

c Listen again, and complete the interviewer's questions:

.... all year round?

.... on the farm too?

2 Ask questions about your partner's lifestyle. Find out if he/she

- reads a newspaper
- listens to the radio
- eats a big breakfast
- drinks coffee
- plays chess
- reads poetry

Now ask two questions of your own.

2 Quiz cards

Wh- questions

National customs
When do the Chinese celebrate New Year?

People and jobs
What does a butcher do?

The Natural World
Where do penguins live?

The arts
Where do people play the *balalaika*?

Food and drink
Where does *couscous* come from?

National customs
What do the Americans celebrate on 4th July?

The Natural World
What do pandas eat?

The arts
Why do people visit the Prado in Madrid?

Use the table to make some quiz questions of your own.

What Where When Why	do does	.... ?

3 When do you wear ...?

Frequency expressions

1 Which words show how often people wear ties?

A
I never wear a tie.

B
I don't wear a tie very often, but I sometimes wear one on special occasions.

C
I only wear a tie at weddings.

D
I always wear a tie at work but I don't usually wear one at home.

E
I usually wear a tie for business, and I often wear one when I go out in the evenings.

You will hear three people talking about when they wear a tie. Match each person with one of the bubbles above.

2 Now talk about yourselves.
When do you wear ...
... a hat?   ... gloves?   ... glasses?
... shorts?   ... make-up?

4 Cultural differences

Choose one of these three short texts about British customs.

'Full English Breakfast'

Many hotels serve what they call 'full English breakfast'. First they bring you cereal and fruit juice, then you get egg, bacon and tomato, and then toast and marmalade. In fact, few people in Britain eat such a big breakfast. It's more normal to have just one of these things, with a cup of tea or coffee. Nowadays, a lot of people start the day with muesli or yoghurt.

Happy New Year

On New Year's Eve, most people in Britain stay up until midnight. They often go to parties, or gather in public places to 'see the New Year in'. At  12 o'clock they wish each other a Happy New Year and sing Auld Lang Syne. After midnight many people visit friends and neighbours; traditionally, they take a piece of coal as a gift. Of course, not everyone goes out: a lot of people stay at home and watch the celebrations on TV. On New Year's Day, people make New Year Resolutions, which they usually forget after a few days.

Presents and cards

There are certain days when people in Britain give presents and send cards. At Christmas, nearly everyone sends cards to friends and relations, and the Post Office employs extra staff to deliver them all. You also receive cards and presents on your birthday. People buy cards for other occasions too: these include Valentine's Day, Mother's Day, Father's Day, Easter and wedding anniversaries. It's common to give flowers on Mother's Day and chocolate eggs at Easter.

What happens in your country?
What are the differences?
Does everyone do the same?

Grammar Checklist

Present simple tense

Third person singular: add **-s** *or* **-es**

I play; they wash; we carry
He plays; she washes; he carries

Negatives

don't/doesn't + *infinitive*

They **don't live** in London.
She **doesn't live** in London.
    (*not* ... ~~doesn't lives~~ ...)

Yes/no questions

Questions: **Do/Does** + *subject* + *infinitive*
Short answers: repeat **do/does** (+ **n't**)

Do you **play** chess?   Yes, I **do**.
                                (*not* ~~Yes, I play.~~)
Does he **play** chess?   No, he **doesn't**.

Wh- questions

Wh- *word* + **do/does** + *subject* + *infinitive*

Where **do** you **live**? (*not* ~~Where you live?~~)
Where **does** he **live**? (*not* ~~Where he lives?~~)

Frequency expressions

Normal position: before the **main** *verb.*

I **usually** wear make-up (*not* ~~I wear usually~~ ...)
She **only** works in the morning.
I don't **often** go out.
    (*or* I don't go out **very often**.)
    (*not* ~~I often don't go out.~~)

See also Reference section, page 131.

Focus on Form

1 Third person -s

play   carry   drive   fly
go   wash   sit   watch
dance   do   teach   make

Add third person -s to these verbs. Use three of them in sentences of your own.

2 Negatives

It's Bill's birthday next week, but he's hard to please.

A Let's get him a novel.
B No – he doesn't read novels.
A What about a bottle of wine?
B No – he doesn't drink wine.

Now you carry on. Start with these ideas:

a some cigars   d a box of chocolates
b a hat   e some theatre tickets
c a swimsuit   f some writing paper

It's Bill and Annie's wedding anniversary next month. Talk about them in the same way.

3 Yes/no questions

Work in threes.

Start with these ideas:

a drive a car?   e eat meat?
b play the piano?   f go to church?
c like cheese?   g like cats?
d speak German?   h work at the weekend?

4 Wh- questions

Where   What   When   Why   How many

The sentences below are about your partner. Ask him/her questions to find the missing information.

a X comes from …
b X lives in …
c X gets up at …
d X eats … for breakfast.
e X has … brothers and sisters.
f X wants to learn English because …

5 Frequency

(not) usually   (not) often   always
sometimes   never

Add a frequency expression to each sentence, so that it is true for you.

Examples:
I always get up late on Sundays.
I don't usually get up late on Sundays.

a I get up late on Sundays.
b I get to work on time.
c I walk to class.
d I read in bed.
e I sleep in the afternoon.
f I make my own bed.
g I sleep with the window open.
h I make New Year Resolutions.

6 Pronunciation

How do you say the words and phrases below?

a helps   thinks   asks
  lives   sings   holds
  catches   pushes   kisses

b Do you speak Spanish?
  Where do you live?

c Does she read a lot?
  When does the train leave?
  He doesn't work here any more.

d They usually get up early.
  I often see them at weekends.

▶ Now listen and check your answers.

4 Going places

1 Public transport

1 Which forms of public transport do you use? Which do you use most?

2 Choose one kind of transport, and complete the table. Which statements do you think are true? Write ✓ or ✗.

   Discuss your answers with your partner.

Form of transport:	✓ or ✗
a They're comfortable.	
b They usually come on time.	
c They're expensive.	
d They're often crowded.	
e You don't have to wait long.	
f They're slow.	
g It's an enjoyable way to travel.	
h It's a safe way to travel.	

2 On the move

📼 You will hear six short scenes. What happens in each one? Use the words in the box.

fill	check in	driver	baggage
land	drive off	ticket	platform
pay	get in	seat	passenger
stop	get on	petrol	stewardess

3 How to get there

1 Three people say how they get from Washington to New York. Fill the gaps with words from the box.

costs	reaches	gets
takes	leaves	arrives

What's the best thing about
– the bus? – the plane? – the train?

A

> I usually fly. If I leave home at 6.30, I can catch the 7.30 a.m. flight, which .... to La Guardia Airport at about 8.30. I'm in the centre of New York by 9.15 so the whole journey .... less than 3 hours. It's expensive – it .... about $300 return – but it's very quick. And there's a plane every hour.

B

> I usually take the Greyhound bus. It .... Washington at 9 a.m., and .... in New York at 1.40 in the afternoon. The New York bus terminal is in Manhattan, so it's very convenient, and it only .... about $85 return on weekdays.

C

> I usually go by train, because it's only a bit slower than the plane and it's more reliable. It's about $100 return. The journey .... about 4 hours. I usually catch the 10.30 train, which .... New York at 10 past 2. It's comfortable, and it's always on time.

2 You're at a tourist information office.

Student A: You're a tourist. Choose a place where you want to go. Find out how to get there.

Student B: You work at the tourist information office. Answer A's questions.

> How can I get to …?

> How much does it cost?

> How long does it take?

4 Airport

READING

1 **Fill the gaps with numbers from the box. Then check your answers in the text.**

14
30
85
1000
9,200
23,500
53,000
74,000
3,000,000
57,000,000
500,000,000

  a Heathrow airport handles over .... items of baggage every year.
  b More than .... people work at Heathrow airport.
  c Every day around .... planes take off and land at Heathrow.
  d Around .... litres of aviation fuel are used every day.
  e Heathrow's police station has .... dogs that can smell drugs.
  f The duty-free shops sell .... cigarettes every year.
  g Every year, around .... people die of heart attacks travelling to or through Heathrow.
  h .... cups of tea and coffee are served in the airport every day.
  i There are .... baggage trolleys for passengers to use.
  j If 10 cm of snow falls, staff have to clear .... tons of snow.
  k You can fly direct from Heathrow to .... countries.

2 **Which of these remarks are true?**

  a 'They have to keep washing the runways.'
  b 'Birds aren't a problem to modern aircraft.'
  c 'If you're in a small plane, you shouldn't fly too close behind a jumbo jet.'
  d 'If a plane can't lower its wheels, it has to land on the grass beside the runway.'
  e 'There aren't any flights from Heathrow after midnight.'

LISTENING

You will hear four people answering these questions:

> How do you feel when you're in an airport?

> What do you do while you're waiting for your flight?

1 **How does each person feel?**

2 **What does each person do? Choose activities from the list.**

> read
> have a meal
> watch other people
> have a drink in the bar
> sit near the departures board
> go to sleep
> wander around
> listen to music
> watch the planes
> talk to people
> go to the duty-free shops

3 **Imagine you're going on a plane journey. Which speaker would you most like to travel with?**

Welcome to Heathrow

LONDON'S HEATHROW IS THE BUSIEST international airport in the world. It handles over 350,000 international flights every year – about 41 million passengers. Around 54,000 people work at Heathrow, roughly the population of a country town.

Huge machines wash the airport's three runways and clear away the oil left by jet engines. Burst tyres can cause a crash, so special trucks continuously check the runways and pick up any loose pieces of metal.

Birds can cause crashes if they get pulled into the engines, and staff work day and night to keep them away from the runways. Their trucks have loudspeakers which send out bird alarm calls and they also use guns with blank cartridges to frighten the birds away.

In the control tower, 150 air traffic controllers bring the planes in and send them off safely. As a plane comes in to land, it normally keeps a distance of five or six kilometres from the planes in front and behind, but in the case of large

Amazing facts ...

- Every year Heathrow handles over 57,000,000 items of baggage.
- There are 9,200 baggage trolleys for passengers – more than at any other airport.
- Airport cafés and bars serve over 23,500 cups of coffee and tea and 11,500 sandwiches every day.
- Heathrow's duty-free shops sell 500 million cigarettes every year.
- For every 10 cm of snow falling on the airport, staff have to remove 74,000 tons of snow to keep the airport open.
- Heathrow averages around 1000 take-offs and landings every day – that's about one per minute from 6 am till midnight.
- 3,000,000 litres of aviation fuel are used every day.
- 70 airlines use Heathrow. They fly direct to 214 destinations in 85 countries.

jumbo jets, the distance behind has to be 10 kilometres. The air turbulence behind these planes can send a small plane out of control.

Near the centre of the airport is the police station. It has a huge picture board of known world terrorists, 14 dogs that can smell drugs and 300 police officers.

There is an aircraft alert almost every day. This happens every time an aircraft lands with one engine shut down or if the pilot cannot lower the plane's wheels. The emergency services can lay a carpet of foam on the runway in less than four minutes.

The Medical Centre has eight nurses and three doctors always on standby. The most common illness is heart attack. Every year about 30 people die in this way while travelling to or through Heathrow.

Because of the noise, only a few flights are permitted between midnight and six in the morning. So during the night Heathrow Airport has its most welcome visitor of all – silence.

1 How do you know?

Present continuous tense

1 Look at the picture.
Is it breakfast time or lunch time?
How do you know?

It's probably breakfast time because ...
... the woman's eating toast.
... the man's eating a roll and butter.
... they're drinking coffee.
... they're not having lunch.
... the people opposite are opening their shop.

Now answer these questions.
How do you know?

a Are they in Britain or in France?
b Is the weather hot or cold?
c Are the man and woman friends?
d Is the man on holiday?
e Is the woman on holiday?

2 Think of two or three replies for each of these situations. Example:

What are you doing? Writing a letter?
No. Actually ...
... I'm writing a poem.
... I'm drawing.
... I'm doing my homework.

a Hurry up! We'll be late!
I won't be a moment. ...
b Where are the children? Are they in bed?
No. ...
c I've got something to tell you.
Shh! ...
d What's he doing up that ladder?
I'm not sure. I think ...
e Hello. Is this a bad time to phone?
Well, it is, actually. ...
f What's that terrible noise next door?
I don't know. Perhaps ...

2 Around now

Present continuous & simple • Question forms

A I don't watch television, but I read a lot in the evenings. At the moment I'm reading a novel by Doris Lessing, called *The Golden Notebook* …

B You wouldn't believe how busy I am at the moment. David and Joyce are on holiday, and I'm looking after the grandchildren while they're away. It's such hard work! I'm missing all my favourite TV programmes …

C It's really boring here at the moment. Everyone's away, so I'm not doing much. I'm just sitting around reading and watching TV …

D I usually read a lot, but just now I'm not reading anything. I'm far too busy. I'm working overtime every night …

1 Look at the activities in the table. Which people usually do them? Which are doing them at the moment? Write letters A, B, C or D in the table.

2 Interview your partner. Mark his/her answers in the table.

	Usually		Around now	
	yes	no	yes	no
Read				
Watch TV				
Work				

3 The whole picture

There is/are + -ing

1 Each of these pictures is part of a larger photo. In the first picture:

– there's someone standing in the water.
– there are some people sitting on the beach.

On the tape three people imagine what there is in the rest of the photo.
What do they say?

2 Choose one of the other pictures and talk about it in the same way.

4 Cartoons

1 Say what's happening in the cartoon.
Use the words in the box to help you.

What do you think the man's saying?
Write a caption for the cartoon.

robber	ticket office
gun	tap
queue	shoulder

2 Look at your own cartoon in the back of the book, and practise describing it. Then describe it to a student from another group.

Grammar Checklist

Present continuous tense

Form of **be** + **-ing**

He's working hard.(*not* ~~He working hard.~~)
They're having lunch.

-ing ending

Short vowels: run → running (*not* ~~runing~~)
Long vowels + e: make → making
   (*not* ~~makeing~~)

Negatives

Add **not**

They're **not** having lunch.

Short forms: I'm not
         They're not / They aren't
         She's not / She isn't

Yes/no questions

Change order: **be** + *subject* + **-ing**
   1   2   3   2   1   3
They're having lunch. → Are they having lunch?

Short answers: Yes, they are. No, they aren't. etc.

Wh- questions

Wh- *word* + **be** + *subject* + **-ing**

What **are** you doing?
   (*not* ~~What you are doing~~?)

There is/are + -ing

There's a man standing at the gate.
   (= There's a man[. He's] standing at the gate.)

See also Reference section, page 132.

Focus on Form

1 Ending with -ing

sell	run	drive	fly
wash	sit	make	buy
send	cut	dance	go

Add -ing to these verbs. Use three of them in sentences of your own.

2 Present continuous

What differences can you find between the couples in the pictures?

Example: the As and the Bs.

The As are drinking coke; the Bs are drinking coffee.

The As are wearing glasses; the Bs aren't (wearing glasses).

Mrs A is wearing a skirt; Mrs B is wearing trousers.

a the Cs and the Es   *c* the As and the Fs
b the Ds and the Hs   *d* the Bs and the Gs

Now choose people in the pictures, and describe them. Your partner must say who they are.

Example: She's wearing glasses, she isn't reading, she's eating and she's drinking orange.

Answer: Mrs F

3 Yes/no questions

Choose people and places from the table.

a man		bathroom
		kitchen
a woman	in the	garden
		bedroom
some children		living room

Student A: Think of an action and write a sentence.

Others: Ask questions and try to guess the sentence.

Example:

He's washing his hair.

A It's a man. He's in the bathroom.
B Is he cleaning his teeth?
A No he isn't.
C Is he having a bath?
A No.
B Is he washing his face?
A No. Not his face.
C Is he washing his hair?
A That's right. He's washing his hair.

Mr & Mrs A   Mr & Mrs B

Mr & Mrs C   Mr & Mrs D

Mr & Mrs E   Mr & Mrs F

Mr & Mrs G   Mr & Mrs H

4 Pronunciation

How do you say the words and phrases below?

a We're having lunch.
They're playing football.

b He isn't feeling very well.
You aren't listening.

c Are you enjoying yourselves?
The children are watching TV.
What are you doing?

d She's working very hard at the moment.
Actually, I'm just washing my hair

🔲 **Now listen and check your answers.**

6 Food and drink

1 Shopping list

1 Which shops sell the things in the list?
What else do the shops sell?
Write three things for each shop.

2 You're going to make a dish (e.g. a stew, a cake, a salad). Write a shopping list.

Show your list to another student. Can he/she guess what you're going to make?

Shopping list

carrots
kilo of lamb
eggs
packet of rice
6 oranges
onions
coffee
large loaf

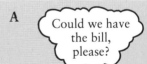

A Could we have the bill, please?

B What would you like to drink?

C Mm. That was a lovely meal.

2 National dishes

1 Read these descriptions of Korean dishes, and match them with the pictures.

Which *two* would you choose?

1 *Oi-naengch'ae*

Oi-naengch'ae is a kind of soup. It is made from cucumbers and onions, and it also has sugar and vinegar in it. You eat it cold.

2 *Paeksolgi*

For this dish you need rice, beans and sugar. You cook the rice and beans and make them into a kind of cake. You serve it cold with fruit.

3 *Poggumbap*

Poggumbap is a rice dish which is very popular in Korea. The rice is fried with small pieces of crab and pork. It is served hot.

4 *Pindaeddok*

These are Korean pancakes. They are made from beans and flour, and also have meat and cabbage in them. You can eat them hot or cold.

5 *Shinsollo*

This is a kind of stew. It is made from different kinds of meat cooked with vegetables, nuts and spices. You serve it in a large pot which you put in the middle of the table.

2 You're planning a special meal for some foreign visitors. Write a menu and include
– a starter
– a main course
– a dessert
– drinks

Explain to your guests what each dish is.

3 Eating out

1 What's happening in the pictures below? Put the remarks in the right order.

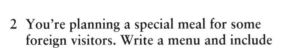 Now listen to the tape and check your answers.

2 Work in threes. Act out a scene in a restaurant.

D	E	F	G
I'll have the chicken, please.	Have you reserved a table?	Are you ready to order now?	What about this table by the window?

Have you got a healthy heart?

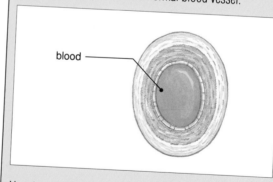

How many of these statements are true of you?

♥ I'm male

♥ Other members of my family have had heart disease

♥ I smoke

♥ I don't do much exercise

♥ I need to lose weight

♥ I've got a high level of cholesterol in my blood

Each *true* is a possible problem for your heart.

READING

Heart disease kills millions of people every year.
What are your chances?

Rate per 100 000

| 200 | 100 | 0 | 100 | 200 | 300 | 400 | 500 | 600 |

Northern Ireland
Scotland
Finland
Czechoslovakia
Ireland
Hungary
England & Wales
New Zealand
Norway
Denmark
Australia
Sweden
United States
Canada
Poland
Netherlands
Germany FRG
Austria
Israel
Germany GDR
Romania
Belgium
Yugoslavia 1983
Italy 1983
Switzerland
Greece
Spain
Portugal 1982
France
Japan

WOMEN

MEN

Deaths from coronary heart disease. The table shows rates of death for men and women aged 40–69 in 1985. A major cause is high levels of cholesterol in the blood.

What is cholesterol?

Cholesterol is a kind of fat. Everyone has some cholesterol in their blood. But if you have a lot, it can give you heart disease.

The problem lies in the blood vessels, which take blood to and from the heart. Here is a normal blood vessel:

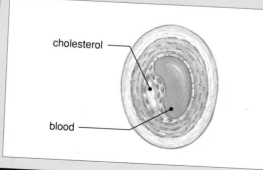

blood

Here is a blood vessel lined with cholesterol. Sooner or later, there will be a problem.

cholesterol

blood

For less cholesterol...

Eat lots of vegetables and fruit.

Olive oil is very good for you. Eating olive oil actually lowers your level of blood cholesterol. (Which countries in the table eat a lot of olive oil?)

Fish oils are also good for your heart. (Look at Japan in the table.)

Exercise helps to lower the level of cholesterol in your blood.

For more cholesterol...

Most kinds of red meat contain a lot of saturated fat.

Butter, milk and cheese contain saturated fat, too.

So does

CHOCOLATE

The yolks of eggs are high in cholesterol

Shellfish are high in cholesterol.

Most vegetable oils are OK, but some may be high in saturated fat.

LISTENING

You will hear two people talking about what they eat and how they live.

1 Listen and complete the table. Write ✓ or ✗.

2 How healthy are they? Give each person a score out of 10.

    1 = *very unhealthy*
    5 = *average*
    10 = *very healthy*

Do they ...	1	2
... feel healthy?		
... smoke?		
... eat healthy food?		
... do a lot of exercise?		
Score:		

1

You're in a strange town, and you want to stay a few days. You go to the Tourist Information Office. Think of three questions to ask.

2

You meet someone at a party, and you want to know more about him or her. Think of three questions to ask.

3

An old friend asks you 'What are you doing these days?' Think of three things you might say.

4

Talk about one of these topics. Can you keep talking for one minute?

neighbours

your favourite drink(s)

airports

restaurants

your home town

travelling by bus

a street you know well

your daily routine

brothers and sisters

love

5 How good?

1 A good student ...

... always comes to class.
... pays attention.
... does homework every day.
... never interrupts the teacher.
... asks intelligent questions.
... doesn't forget things.

Do you agree?

2 Work in pairs. Choose one of the following, and discuss what the person does and doesn't do. Write a list.

a good mother	a good father
a good wife	a good husband
a good friend	a good son or daughter
a good boss	a good employee

Show your list to other students.

6 Having a wonderful time

Engadine, Soglio

Here we are in the Alps!
The weather's good and
we're getting up really
early – about 5 o'clock –
and climbing all day.
We can't afford to eat
in restaurants, so we're
living on bread and
cheese – but otherwise
we're having a
wonderful time.
love J & N

A. Davidson
2 Portobello Crescent
London W14

England

© Cartes Postales Suisses

1 Imagine you're on holiday.

a What kind of holiday is it?
b Where are you?
c What's the weather like?
d How are you spending your time?
e Are you enjoying yourself?

2 Write a postcard to a friend.

7 The past

1 Famous firsts

Past simple tense

1 Fill the gaps in text A using verbs from the box.

arrived	didn't arrive
ate	didn't eat
drank	didn't drink
flew	didn't fly
had	didn't have
left	didn't leave
took	didn't take

A

When Charles Lindbergh ..... from New York to Paris in 1927 on the first solo non-stop flight across the Atlantic, he ..... much food with him. He ..... New York in his plane 'Spirit of St Louis' with several bottles of water and five sandwiches. During the flight he ..... the water but he ..... all the sandwiches – he still ..... three of them when he ..... in Paris 33 hours later.

2 Now complete the other three texts. Use past tense forms of the verbs in the box below.

be	cut	invent	say
break	explode	kill	take
come	go	know	throw
crash	have	like	use

B

When Joseph Merlin ..... roller skates in 1760, he decided to demonstrate them at a large party. Half way through the party, he ..... into the ballroom wearing his skates and playing a violin. Unfortunately he ..... how to turn or stop, and he ..... into a large mirror at the end of the room. He ..... the mirror and his violin, and ended up in hospital.

C

In 1868, the City Council set up the world's first traffic light outside the Houses of Parliament in London. The traffic light ..... electricity – instead it ..... gas lamps behind red and green glass. It ..... a great success: after a few days it ..... and ..... a policeman. It was almost 50 years before they built another traffic light.

D

A customer in an expensive New York restaurant complained to head waiter George Crum that he ..... his chips because they were too thick. Crum ..... very annoyed. He ..... into the kitchen, ... a potato into very thin slices, and ..... the slices into a pan of hot oil. Then he ..... them back to the customer, who (to Crum's surprise) ..... that they tasted delicious. They ..... the world's first potato crisps.

3 Work in pairs. Write the first sentence of a story. Then pass it to another pair to continue.

---

2 Getting the details

1 You'll hear someone telling some friends about a recent journey to Austria.

 Where? stop? Vienna?

a What questions do you think his friends ask? When?

How? good time?

b 📼 Listen to the conversation. What were the questions? What answers does he give?

2 Think of questions you might ask if someone tells you

a I went camping last weekend.
b It was my birthday yesterday.
c I took a holiday job in the summer.

Now choose one of the situations and act out a conversation.

3 Aesop's fables

The Grasshopper and the Ants

A grasshopper spent the summer singing and dancing in the sun. One day he saw an ant hurrying by. She looked very tired and hot.

'Why are you working on such a lovely day?' asked the grasshopper.

'I'm collecting food for the winter,' said the ant, and went on her way. She joined all the other ants carrying food to their store. The grasshopper sang another song and carried on dancing.

When winter came and there was snow on the ground, the grasshopper had nothing to eat. He was very hungry, so he went and asked the ants to give him some food.

'We worked all summer to collect our food. What did you do?' said one of the ants.

'I was busy singing and dancing,' replied the grasshopper.

'Well, if you sing and dance all summer and do no work,' said the ant, 'then you must starve in the winter.'

Moral: ▓▓▓▓▓▓▓▓▓▓▓▓▓▓▓

1 Choose the best moral for the story.

a People who plan ahead are often selfish.
b If you're in trouble, no one will help you.
c A short happy life is better than a long boring one.
d Always prepare for difficult times in the future.
e Artists aren't important in society.

2 Read your own story in the back of the book. Then tell it to another student. Can he/she guess the moral?

4 When did it happen?

The train left at 7 o'clock.

It snowed at the weekend.

The letter arrived on Saturday.

The baby's a Gemini. She was born on 3rd June.

The President resigned in May.

His plays were very popular in the thirties.

Elvis Presley died in 1977.

Don't talk to him. He gave up smoking this morning.

They got married the day before yesterday.

Did you see the match last Wednesday?

I started evening classes last week.

1 When do we use

– *at?*
– *on?*
– *in?*
– no preposition?

Change each sentence using *ago*. Example:

They got married the day before yesterday.
They got married *two days ago*.

2 How good is your memory?
When did you last

– go to the hairdresser?
– lose your temper?
– have a cup of coffee?
– laugh?
– cook a meal?
– drink champagne?
– write a letter?
– go to the dentist?
– sing a song in public?

Grammar Checklist

Past simple tense

Regular verbs: add **-ed** *or* **-d**
stay – stay**ed**; live – liv**ed**; carry – carri**ed**
Irregular verbs: see list on page 143.

Negatives

didn't + *infinitive*
We went to the party. →
We **didn't go** to the party.
(*not* ... ~~didn't went~~ ...)

Yes/no questions

Did + *subject* + *infinitive*
He went home. → **Did** he **go** home?
Short answers: Yes, he **did**. No, he **didn't**.
(*not* ~~Yes, he went~~.)

Wh- questions

Wh- *word* + **did** + *subject* + *infinitive*
Where **did** you **stay**? (*not* ~~Where you stayed~~?)

Time prepositions

at: at 6 o'clock, at midday
on: on Monday, on 3rd April
in: in the morning, in May, in spring, in 1920
(*no preposition:* last year, yesterday)

ago

I met him two years **ago**.
(*not* ... ~~before two years.~~)

See also Reference section, page 133.

Focus on Form

1 Regular past forms

wait	arrive	play	carry	stop
wash	invite	enjoy	try	plan

What are the past forms of these verbs? Use three of them in sentences of your own.

2 Irregular past forms

Student A: Choose a verb from the box and make a sentence in the past. Say *buzzed* instead of the verb you chose.

Student B: Give the past tense of the missing verb.

see	write	eat	bring	wear
tell	wake	drink	buy	go
take	fly	leave	read	drive
make	give	have	come	get
lose	find	meet	sing	break

Examples:

A Yesterday I *buzzed* a good film.
B saw
A One day she *buzzed* a gold coin in her garden.
B found

3 Positive & negative

Choose another student in the class. Imagine three things he/she did yesterday, and three things he/she didn't do yesterday. Write them down. Examples:

You had coffee for breakfast.
You sang a song.

You didn't cook a meal.
You didn't kiss anyone.

Read them out and see if you were right.

4 Past tense questions

Choose one of the stories in the newspaper column above, and make past tense questions about it. Examples:

When did Marie Turpin get married?
Where did she get married?
Did the bridegroom wear a tie?

Now see if other students can answer your questions.

■ P E O P L E ■

Wet wedding

OLYMPIC SWIMMER Marie Turpin got married last Friday – under water. The wedding took place in a swimming pool in Melbourne.

Marie wore a white dress, but bridegroom Jack wore just a swimsuit. Guests sat on chairs around the pool as the Rev. Kenneth Cook – himself a good swimmer – jumped in the water to marry the couple. They later left for a honeymoon in Fiji – by boat.

Royal visit

MRS VIOLET MACKENZIE had a surprise visitor for tea on Wednesday – the Prince of Wales.

'The doorbell rang at about 4 o'clock,' said Mrs MacKenzie, who lives in South London. 'I opened the door, and there was the Prince. He asked if he could use the phone, so I invited him in and gave him a cup of tea.'

The Prince called on Mrs MacKenzie after his car broke down on the way to Heathrow airport.

'It was the nearest house,' he said. 'Mrs MacKenzie was very kind.'

Dangerous pet

TOP FASHION MODEL Gina Riccardi cried last week when she said goodbye to her pet – a young Siberian wolf called Sasha. She kept the wolf in her Rome apartment, took it for walks in the park, and even took it shopping with her. 'People were terrified,' complained a neighbour. 'I took a gun with me whenever I went out.'

Last week, police told Ms Riccardi that she had to give the wolf up. She gave it to a local zoo.

5 Pronunciation

How do you say the words and phrases below?

a stayed   arrived   used
stopped   watched   asked
wanted   waited   landed

b Did you have a good time?
When did you arrive?

c We didn't like it very much.

d at nine o'clock this morning
yesterday afternoon
a few days ago

🔲 Now listen and check your answers.

8 Somewhere to live

1 Houses

A We've just moved to a house in the suburbs. It's got three bedrooms and a large garden. It's very spacious and there's lots of room for the children. The living room faces south, so it's quite sunny.

B I've got a 4-room flat in a big block near the city centre. It's on the 5th floor, and has a lovely view of the park. It's very convenient for the shops, too. Unfortunately it's on a main road, so it's a bit noisy.

C They've also got a little cottage in the country. It's in a lovely position, right on the edge of a small lake, but it doesn't get much sun, so it's rather dark inside.

D I've found a quiet little flat in the old part of the town. It's a bit small – just 2 rooms – but it's got a balcony which looks out on a square.

1 Match the descriptions with the pictures. Complete the table.

	What type?	*Where is it?*	*More about its position*
A			faces south
B	flat		
C		in the country	
D			
Your home			

2 Describe your home (or somebody else's).

2 Rooms and furniture

1 Look at the items in the box. Which rooms do they go in? Which can go in any room?

Think of other things that can go in each room.

armchair	cupboard	shower
bookshelf	curtains	sink
carpet	desk	wardrobe
cooker	mirror	washbasin

2 Now think of one luxury item to put in each room.

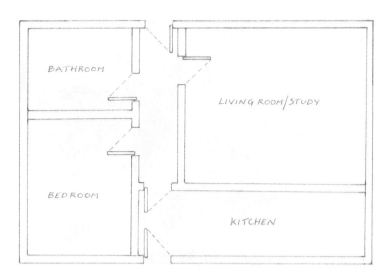

3 Personal space

1 [cassette icon] Look at the first room. You'll hear three people talking about it.

What do they like about it? What don't they like? What changes would they make?

Do you agree?

2 What do you think of the other rooms? Say what changes you'd make.

4 Haunted houses

READING

What do you know about ghosts? Here's some basic information.

Everyone's Guide to ... *HAUNTED HOUSES*

Haunted houses are usually large, old and gloomy. They're often empty, or have some rooms that aren't used.	Usually someone died a tragic death in the house: this person appears as a ghost.	Ghosts are unhappy. They haunt the house because they can't rest. They always appear in the same part of the house – usually the room where they died.
Ghosts usually appear at night. They wear old-fashioned clothes, and they don't say anything.	Some ghosts carry things, like knives, books or even their own heads.	Some ghosts don't appear at all. They just make a knocking or banging noise.	If you see a ghost, don't panic. They're usually quite harmless, and some are friendly.

1 **Read about Sandford Orcas Manor. Is it a typical haunted house?**

2 **Complete the table.**

3 **Find the four ghosts of Sandford Orcas Manor.**

Which ghost?	He killed ...	You can see him in ...
1 previous owner		
2	visitors	
3		the corridors
4		

a   c   d   e   f   g

b

SANDFORD ORCAS MANOR

Dorset, England

Next to the church in the village of Sandford Orcas there is an old gatehouse. If you go through the gate you arrive at the sinister manor house which is famous for its large number of ghosts.

The present owner of the manor says that it is difficult to keep servants because the ghosts frighten them. Many people have seen the ghost of the previous owner. He was a farmer who committed suicide by hanging himself from the gatehouse, and he often appears in the garden wearing old working clothes.

Another ghost is an 18th century priest who used to kill visitors while they were asleep in their beds. He still sometimes frightens guests in the middle of the night by standing over their beds holding a knife.

The ghost of a servant sometimes walks along the dark corridors of the house. He murdered his master at Sandford Orcas, but nobody knows why.

But perhaps the most frightening story is of a young man who grew up in the house and then became a sailor. While he was at sea, he killed a boy, and then went mad. When he returned to Sandford Orcas, they locked him in a room at the back of the house. He never left the room again, and died there several years later. On some nights when the moon is full, you can hear him screaming and banging on the door of the room.

LISTENING

⌨ On the tape, a man talks about something that happened when he was a child.

1 Listen to the first part of the story, and complete the table. Write T or F.

   What do you think the neighbours said?

2 Now listen to the end of the story.
   Were you right?

True or False?	T/F
a The boy was six years old.	
b He was with his mother.	
c He saw an old woman in the cellar.	
d She had black hair.	
e She had a coloured apron.	
f His mother saw her too.	
g He stayed and talked to her.	
h His parents told the neighbours about it.	

1 Find the differences

some • any

1 🔲 You will hear two people talking about a picture. Is it the same as the picture on this page?

Write down two things they say:

a using *some*
b using *any*

2 Work in pairs.

Student A: Look at the picture on page 114.
Student B: Look at the picture on page 116.

Ask about your partner's picture, and talk about your own. Try to find eight differences.

2 Questions of quantity

Quantity expressions • How much/many?

1 **What can you say about these people?**
   Use expressions from the table.

   – a busy person
   – a lonely person
   – a rich person
   – a poor person
   – a popular person

not any	friends
not much /not many	money
quite a lot of	spare time
a lot of	etc.

   What questions could you ask about them using
   How much? **and** *How many?*

2 **How much do you know about yourself?**
   How many of these questions can you answer?

   a How many books have you got in your living room?
   b Exactly how much money do you have with you at the moment?
   c How many hours did you spend watching TV last week?
   d How many teeth have you got?
   e How many times have you looked in the mirror today?

   Now write two questions of your own. Ask other students.

3 What's the problem?

too much/many • not enough

Cut milk production, Minister tells farmers

by our staff reporter

The Minister of Agriculture yesterday told farmers' representatives that the EEC was producing far too much milk. Speaking at a luncheon given by leaders of the Farmers' Union at their headquarters in London, Mr Arkwright called for an end to Europe's butter mountain and milk lake. Quoting the latest scientific evidence that too many cows contribute towards the Greenhouse Effect, he went on to say that radical changes would have to be made in the course of the next few

We're producing too much milk.

There are too many cows.

People aren't drinking enough milk.

1 You will hear three extracts from a radio news programme. Match each one with a suitable headline. What problems does each speaker mention?

Eat less junk food, doctors warn

Village school closes

We can't live on my wages, says father of 8 children

Government to build 500,000 new houses in cities

London traffic – it's getting worse!

Nurses ask for more pay

2 Look at the other headlines, and imagine what the problems are.
   Make sentences with *too much*, *too many* or *not enough*.

4 Points of view

1 Think about TV in your country.
Which opinions do you agree with?

a Well, there's plenty of pop music, but there isn't enough serious music.

b There isn't enough sport – I'd like to see more live matches.

c I think there are too many advertisements.

d Most things are quite good, but I think there should be more religious programmes.

e There are too many old black and white films. I'd like to see more modern films.

g I think there are too many quiz shows and chat shows. I'd like to see more serious programmes.

f The news programmes aren't very good. They don't give enough international news.

	Agree	–	Disagree
a			
b			
c			
d			
e			
f			
g			

2 Compare your answers with your partner's.

Grammar Checklist

Count & non-count nouns

Count nouns: a pen, pens; a chair, chairs
Non-count nouns: money; water; furniture

some & any

some: *positive sentences*
I've got **some** paper.

any: *negatives & questions*
Have you got **any** paper?
I haven't got **any** paper.

much & many

much *with non-count nouns*
many *with count nouns*

We haven't got **much** money.
Do you know **many** people here?

How much/many?

How much coffee is there?
How many eggs are there?
   (*not* How much eggs ...)

too much/many

There are **too many** people here.
   (*not* ... too many of people ...)
There's **too much** traffic.

not enough

There aren't **enough** chairs.
I haven't got **enough** money.
   (*not* ... enough of money.)
   (*not* ... I haven't got money enough.)

See also Reference section, page 134.

Focus on Form

	I've got ...	I haven't got ...	Have you got ... ?
pen	I've got a pen.		
money			Have you got any money?
stamps		I haven't got any stamps.	

1 Some & any

Complete the table above.

Find out what your partner has got.

Example: money

A Have you got any money on you?
B No, I haven't.
  Yes, a bit.
  Yes – I've got about 5 dollars.

Ask about:

a	pen	d	keys	g	matches
b	stamps	e	comb	h	chewing gum
c	string	f	purse		

Now say what your partner's got.

2 How much? & How many?

You know that your partner ...
  ... has more than one sister.
  ... takes sugar in coffee.
  ... speaks several languages.
  ... knows some Swahili.
  ... wants to borrow some money.
  ... watches soap operas.
  ... eats eggs for breakfast.
  ... drinks a lot of milk.

Student A: **Ask questions with** *How much?* **and** *How many?*

Student B: **Give suitable answers.**

3 Too much & too many

Do you eat too much chocolate? Do you read too many romantic novels?

Use the table to talk about your *bad habits*. (If you don't have any bad habits yourself, talk about someone else.)

I	eat watch read drink	too much too many	....

4 Not enough

A I want to have a bath.
B There isn't enough hot water.
A Let's make some chips.
B There aren't enough potatoes.

Have similar conversations.

A wants ...
  ... to make a mushroom omelette.
  ... to have a shower.
  ... a banana milk shake.
  ... to invite some people for dinner.
  ... to wash his/her hair.
  ... to make a fire.
  ... to have some friends to stay.
  ... to go for a drive in the country.

5 Pronunciation

How do you say the words and phrases below?

a There's some cheese in the fridge.
   There are some apples on the plate.

b He's got quite a lot of friends.
   There's plenty of food.

c Have you got any money?
   How many children have you got?

d You don't eat enough fruit.

🔲 **Now listen and check your answers.**

10 Clothes

1 Things to wear

1 In the pictures, find

  – three things you wear on your feet.
  – three things to keep you warm.
  – three things you wear in hot weather.
  – three things that only women wear.

Sort out the pictures. What is each person wearing? Example:

Anna is wearing a red jumper, blue jeans, and sandals.

2 On a piece of paper, write down what you're wearing at the moment. Other students will identify you from your description.

2 Clothes quiz

A B C D E F

1 What are these samples made of?
   Which samples are plain? striped?
   Which have a check pattern? a flowery
   pattern?

2 **Which is the odd one out?**
   – earring   – bracelet
   – belt   – necklace

3 **Which of these people wear a uniform?**
   – soldier   – teacher
   – nurse   – police officer

4 **What happens in between?**
   go to the swimming pool → jump in the water
   have a shower   → go out for the evening
   go into the bedroom → get into bed

5 🔲 **You will hear two people talking
   in a clothes shop. Fill the gaps in their
   conversation with expressions from
   the box.**

   suits you
   buy it
   try it on
   fit
   goes with

3 How clothes conscious are you?

Answer these questions with your partner.
Which of you is more clothes conscious?

1 **When do you like to wear smart clothes?**
   a all the time
   b when you go out
   c only on special occasions

2 **If you pass a clothes shop, do you stop and
   look in the window?**

3 **Think of someone you met yesterday. Can
   you remember what they were wearing?**

4 **You're invited to a wedding. Do you**
   a buy something new to wear?
   b wear what you wore to the last wedding
       you went to?
   c not wear anything special?

5 **'You can tell what people are like by looking
   at their clothes.' Do you agree?**

6 **What do you know about this year's 'look'?
   What are women wearing? What are men
   wearing? What colours are in fashion?**

4 Going for gold

READING

How much do you know about gold? Try to answer these questions. Then check your answers in the text.

1 People first used gold wedding rings
   a in Egypt.
   b in China.
   c in Turkey.
   d in the United States.

2 How much gold ore do you need to make 25 grams of gold?
   a 25 grams
   b 100 grams
   c 5 kilos
   d 3 tons

3 Is gold always the same colour?

4 An 18 carat gold ring is
   a pure gold.
   b 75% gold.
   c 50% gold.
   d 25% gold.

5 The picture below shows a hallmark. What does this tell you?

6 Which of these are harmful to gold?
   – water   – salt
   – soap   – perfume
   – detergent

7 Your great grandmother's gold ring is too small for you. Can you do anything about it?

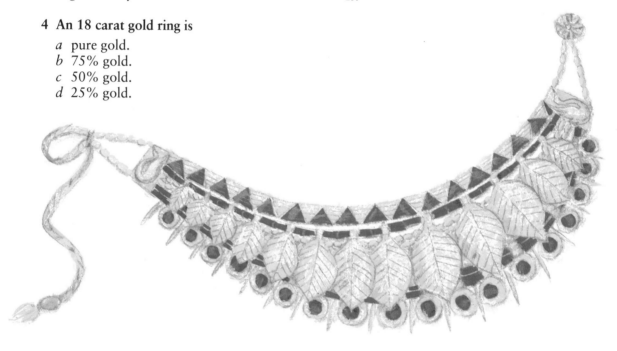

LISTENING

1 Imagine you meet someone wearing this gold pendant. Think of two or three questions to ask about it.

2 ▭ You will hear a woman describing the pendant. Which of your questions does she answer?

3 The woman talks about these things:
   – a market
   – a hallmark
   – an ankh
   – tombs
   – a baby

   Listen again. What does she say about each one?

GOING FOR GOLD

There's nothing nicer than receiving gold as a present. But if you're buying it, follow these golden rules

What to look for

HALLMARKING

This indicates that gold has been tested for quality and that it's up to the correct standard.

A hallmark shows that the article you're buying is made from real gold.

Note: items weighing under one gram, like small earrings, are not hallmarked, so buy these from a reputable jeweller.

> **FACT**
> *The Egyptians were probably the first people to exchange gold wedding rings. The shape of a circle signified continuity and unity while the gold symbolised eternity. The wedding ring is worn on the third finger because it was believed that a vein ran from that finger to the heart!*

CARAT GUIDE

Gold is graded by carats, which show how pure the gold is. The higher the carat number, the more gold there is in the jewellery. So 24 carat = pure gold (99.9 per cent pure – 999 on the hallmark); 22 carat = 22 parts gold to two parts other metals (91.6% pure – 916 on the hallmark);18 carat = 18 parts gold to six parts other metals (75% pure – 750 on the hallmark); nine carat = nine parts gold to 15 parts

alloy (37.5% pure – 375 on the hallmark) as shown above.

Buyers' guide

- When choosing a ring, it's important that it fits correctly. So always ask your jeweller to measure your ring size – he has a gauge with different size holes in it. To decide on your ring size, choose the size that fits tightly but comfortably around your finger.
- Most rings come in a range of sizes. If the ring you want is too big or too small, you can ask the jeweller to alter the size for you.
- Although nine carat gold is the most popular choice, 18 carat is a better buy if you can afford it. It contains twice as much pure gold, and it's also nearer a true gold colour.
- Avoid high fashion designs. Gold lasts for ever, so buy a classic style.
- Ask to see different coloured gold and decide what suits you best. Yellow is the most common (mixed with copper or silver), red (mixed with cadmium and silver) is quite unusual and white (mixed with nickel, zinc or palladium) is a much lighter colour.

> **FACT**
> *Believe it or not, it takes three tons of ore to produce just 25 grams of gold.*

Caring for gold

- Always take off your jewellery before doing housework. Detergents and cleaning powders can make it dull.
- Put jewellery on last when dressing. Perfumes and hairsprays can tarnish it.
- Don't swim when wearing any gold – you might lose it. Also, chlorine and salt water can have a bad effect.
- Clean it regularly. Soak in warm soapy water and gently brush with a toothbrush. Rinse in clean water and dry with a soft, clean cloth.
- To prevent scratching, keep gold separately in a jewellery box.

Future plans

1 Intentions

going to

When I get to the hotel ...

When I get back home ...

When I pass my driving test ...

When I get out of here ...

When the children go to their grandparents ...

When I retire ...

When the holidays start ...

1 Whose thoughts are these? Match the bubbles below with three of the pictures.

A

... I'm going to wear comfortable old clothes, and I'm not going to shave. I'm going to see my girlfriend, and I'm going to go to lots of parties. I'm going to eat lots of good home cooking.

B

... I'm going to take the whole family out. We're going to drive right into the country, and have a picnic by a lake. And in the evening we're going to see a drive-in movie.

C

... I'm going to stay in bed every morning and read the newspaper. I'm not going to cook anything or wash anything. And I'm going to go out every single evening.

**2 Now choose one of the other people and continue his/her thoughts.
Write sentences with *going to* and *not going to*.
Other students will guess whose thoughts they are.**

2 Arrangements

Today is Tuesday 8th May.

1 Look at this person's notice-board.

What's he doing ...
... this evening?
... tomorrow?
... the day after tomorrow?
... next Tuesday?
... in two weeks?
... in two months?

2 What's on your 'notice-board'? Tell your partner what you're doing, and when.

3 I'm not sure yet

1 🔲 You will hear some students talking about what they're going to do when they leave college.
Are they sure what they're going to do? Fill in the table.

	Is he/she going to ...	Sure	Not sure yet
Speaker 1	... work as a nurse in Kenya?		
Speaker 2	... visit her cousin in New York?		
Speaker 3	... work in an office?		
Speaker 4	... have a long holiday?		
Speaker 5	... work in a café?		
Speaker 6	... write a novel?		

2 Answer these questions. If you're sure, use *I'm going to*.
If you're not sure, use *I'll probably* or *I expect I'll*.

What are you going to do ...
... tomorrow night?
... on your next birthday?
... when you retire?

Now make up a question of your own. Ask other students.

4 Round trip

1 Work with a partner. You have one week's holiday. Choose one of the maps and plan a trip. Decide
- where you're going to go.
- how you're going to travel.
- what you're going to do in each place.

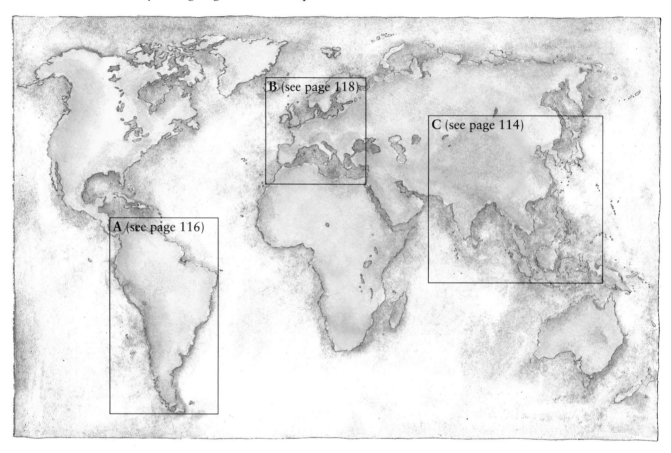

B (see page 118)

C (see page 114)

A (see page 116)

2 Ask other students about their plans, and tell them about yours.

Grammar Checklist

Talking about future plans

going to: *for intentions*
I'm **going to** watch TV this evening.

Present continuous: *for things that are already arranged*
I'm **meeting** some friends tomorrow.

I'll probably/ I expect I'll: *for things you're not yet sure about*
I'll probably just have a sandwich for lunch.
I expect I'll watch TV this evening.

Time expressions
tomorrow, next week, next Thursday
in three days, **in** a year

going to

be (+ **not**) + **going to** + *infinitive*
I'm **going to** watch TV.
Are you **going to** watch TV?
She's **not going to** get a job.

'go' & 'come'

Use Present continuous instead of 'going to go'
and 'going to come'
I'm **going** to the concert.
Are you **coming** to the party?

See also Reference section, page 135.

Focus on Form

1 Going to

Sonia is taking an important exam next month. She's decided to work as hard as she can. Talk about her plans using *going to* and *not going to*.

Examples: She's going to get up early.
She isn't going to watch TV.

– go to parties   – ask her mother to stay
– answer the phone   – do a lot of housework
– read a lot of books – take private lessons
– eat take-away food   – stay up late

2 Present continuous

What activities can you see in the pictures? Write five activities in your diary, leaving two days free.

Mon	
Tues	
Wed	
Thurs	
Fri	
Sat	
Sun	

Talk to your partner. Try to find a day when you're both free to go to the cinema.

Example:

A I can't go on Monday. My parents are coming to dinner. What are you doing on Tuesday?
B I'm babysitting then. Are you free on Friday?

Now try to find someone else who's free to go with you.

3 Arrangements: questions

When?   What?   Where?   Who?
How many?   How much?

Example: I'm playing tennis on ... with ...

A When are you playing tennis?
B (I'm playing tennis) tomorrow afternoon.
A Who are you playing with?
B (I'm playing with) Kate.

Ask (and answer) questions about these arrangements:

We're getting married next ...(1) in a little church in ...(2). We're inviting ...(3) people to the wedding. We're going to ...(4) for our honeymoon.

My father's retiring in ...(5), so my parents are moving to ...(6). They're buying a lovely little house right by the beach. And it's really cheap – they're only paying ...(7).

Tomorrow afternoon I'm ...(8) with ...(9).

4 Pronunciation

How do you say the words and phrases below?

a I'm going to get a new job.
   Where are you going to stay?

b Are you playing tennis tomorrow?
   Who are you playing with?

c I expect we'll go out for a meal.
   I'll probably bring my camera.

Now listen and check your answers.

12 How do you feel?

1 Aches and pains

1 Match the problems with the pictures. What other things could cause the same problems?

I've got a terrible headache.

Ooh. My wrist really hurts.

I've got a terrible stomach ache.

I've got a pain in my chest.

I woke up this morning with a sore throat.

I think I'll sit down. My back aches.

I've got a toothache.

My feet are a bit sore.

2 Work in pairs.

Student A: Choose a problem and decide how you got it.

Student B: Ask some questions to find out more about A's problem.

2 What do you do?

1 What do people do if
  a they have a cold?
  b they feel sick?
  c they can't get to sleep?
  d they have 'flu?
  e they have toothache?
  f they want to lose weight?
  g they have hiccups?

  Choose answers from the box.

take vitamin C
go on a diet
lie down
see a doctor
drink some water
go to the dentist
take an aspirin
count to 100
get some fresh air
go to bed

2 🖭 You will hear four people. Which problems are they talking about? What do they do about them?

Now talk about yourself. What do you do?

3 Going to the doctor

1 **Put the pictures in the right order. Say what's happening in each one, using words from the box.**

prescription	appointment	medicine
doctor	examine	ill
better	questions	chemist's

2 **Write the story. Add any details you like.**

A   B   C

D   E   F

G   H

4 All in the mind

READING

Read the text about the hypochondriac and answer the questions.

1 Which illnesses does the man think he has?
Write ✔ or ✗.

☐ cholera
☐ malaria
☐ hepatitis
☐ yellow fever
☐ housemaid's knee

2 The man first thought
  a his pulse was too fast.
  b his pulse was too slow.
  c his pulse had stopped.

3 The man then thought
  a his heart was too fast.
  b his heart was too slow.
  c his heart had stopped.

4 The man thought
  a his tongue looked normal.
  b something was wrong with his tongue.
  c his tongue wasn't there at all.

5 He doesn't tell the doctor what illnesses he's got because
  a he's not sure.
  b it would take too long.
  c he's frightened.

6 The doctor thinks
  a the man is very ill.
  b the man is slightly ill.
  c the man isn't ill.

7 How is the doctor's prescription unusual?

WRITING

Write a prescription for one of these people.

– someone who is working too hard
– someone who has problems with a boy/girlfriend
– someone who is bored

LISTENING

BBC RADIO FOUR

10.30am
Casebook
Mind and body
In the last of four programmes about doctors at work Kate Ingham talks to psychiatrist Lawrie Reznek about hypochondria.

FM 92.4–94.6 MHz
LW 198 kHz
MW See panel page 72
News 6.00am, 6.30
7.00 LW, 8.00, 9.00, 1.00pm
4.00, 5.00, 6.00, 9.00,
10.00, 12 midnight
Weather 6.03*am, 6.55,
7.55, 8.55, 12.55pm,
5.55 LW, 9.59, 12.30*am
Shipping forecasts
5.55am, 1.55pm LW,
5.50 LW, 12.33am

6.00am News Briefing

Lawrie Reznek

You will hear a psychiatrist answering three questions about hypochondria.

1 Here are the questions and the beginnings of the psychiatrist's replies. How do you think each one continues?

Q1: What is hypochondria?
I think a lot of people get stressed and when you get stressed you get anxious. So for example when you get anxious your heart starts beating faster …

Q2: How can you cure hypochondria?
I think one of the things I would do would be to say to this person 'Look, I think there's a spider crawling up your back' …

Q3: Do doctors suffer from hypochondria?
Yes, I think they're the worst sufferers of hypochondria. All doctors have been medical students …

2 🔲 Now listen to the interview.

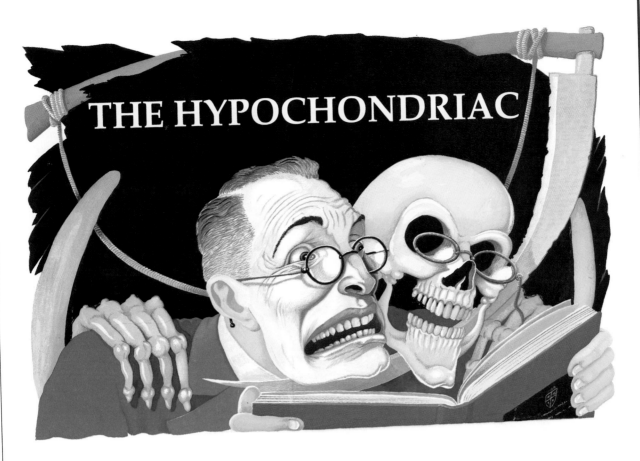

THE HYPOCHONDRIAC

ONE DAY when I was sitting in the local library, I started to read a medical encyclopedia that was lying on the table in front of me.

The first illness I read about was cholera. As I read the list of symptoms, it occurred to me that perhaps I had cholera myself. I sat for a while, too frightened to move. Then, in a kind of dream, I started to turn the pages of the book again. I came to malaria. Yes, there was no doubt about it – I had malaria too. And I certainly had hepatitis. And yellow fever. And so it went on. I read through the whole book, and by the end I came to the conclusion that I had everything. There was only one illness I didn't have – and that was housemaid's knee.

I sat and thought, and I became more and more worried. I wondered how long I had to live. I tried to examine myself. I felt my pulse. At first, I couldn't find it at all; then, suddenly, it seemed to start off. I looked at my watch to time it – it was beating 147 times a minute. I tried to feel my heart. I couldn't feel it. It wasn't beating. I stuck my tongue out and tried to look at it. I could only see the end of it, but from that I was even more certain than before that I had yellow fever.

I went straight to my doctor, who was a good friend of mine.

"What's the matter with you?" he asked.

"Life is short, and you are a busy man," I said. "So I won't tell you what *is* the matter with me. I'll just tell what is *not* the matter with me. I have not got housemaid's knee. Everything else, however, I *have* got." And I told him all about the library and the medical encyclopedia.

Then he opened my mouth and looked at my tongue, and he felt my pulse, and he listened to my heart. Then he sat down and wrote a prescription. It said:

> 3 good meals every day
> 1 two-mile walk every morning
> 1 bed at 11 o'clock every night
> ... and don't read medical books!

I followed the doctor's instructions, and I am happy to say that I now feel quite well again.

Adapted from Three Men in a Boat *by Jerome K. Jerome, first published in 1889.*

Revision and extension

1

You're coming back from a trip abroad, and you're talking to the person sitting next to you. Think of three interesting things to say about your trip.

2

A friend of yours has got a new job. Think of three questions to ask about the job using *How much?* or *How many?*

3

On a train, the person sitting next to you says 'I'm on my way to Madrid'. Think of three questions to ask.

4

Talk about one of these topics. Can you keep talking for one minute?

television

colds

next weekend

your favourite room

jewellery

ghosts

useful things to take on a journey

going to the doctor

shopping

a time when you wore something special

5 The shopping game

1 You work in one of these shops.

vegetable shop
fruit shop
clothes shop
furniture shop
chemist's

Choose a shop, and write down five things you sell.

Shop: ....
1
2
3
4
5

2 Now think of five things you want to buy from other shops.

Write them in the shopping list.

Shopping List
1
2
3
4
5

3 Try to buy the things on your list from the other shops.

How many things did you manage to buy?

6 Guess who?

Students A, B and C: Find out about Student D's life up to the age of 16. Ask about things he/she did, and when he/she did them.

Student D: Answer the other students' questions.

Now choose five things about Student D's life. Write them on a piece of paper, and give it to the teacher to read out. Other students will guess who the person is.

13 Comparison

1 Which is better?

Comparative adjectives • than

1 What are the comparative forms of the words in the box? Examples:
clean → cleaner
helpful → more helpful

cheap	quiet	interesting
clean	lively	comfortable
big	friendly	attractive
good	polite	efficient
much/many	helpful	convenient

Oh the Regal's not bad, but I prefer the Metropole.

Really? Why's that?

I really like my new job. It's much better than my old one.

Is it? In what way?

2 What do you think the people might say about

– the Metropole Hotel?
– the new job?
– the Star disco?

Examples:

The Metropole's cleaner (than the Regal). And the staff are more helpful.

Listen to the conversations. Did you have the same reasons?

I don't go to Maxi's disco any more. The Star's more fun.

The Star? What's so good about it?

2 General knowledge

Comparative adjectives • Which ...?

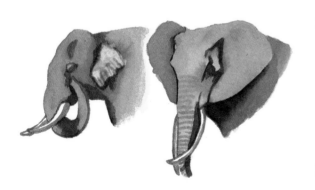

1 Can you answer these questions?

a Which has bigger ears, an African elephant or an Asian elephant?
b Which is further from the Sun, Jupiter or Saturn?
c Which has more calories, 100 grams of butter or 100 grams of olive oil ?
d Which is longer, the River Nile or the River Amazon?
e Which is heavier, a litre of water or a litre of beer?

2 Look at your own facts in the back of the book. What questions can you ask?

3 Outstanding features

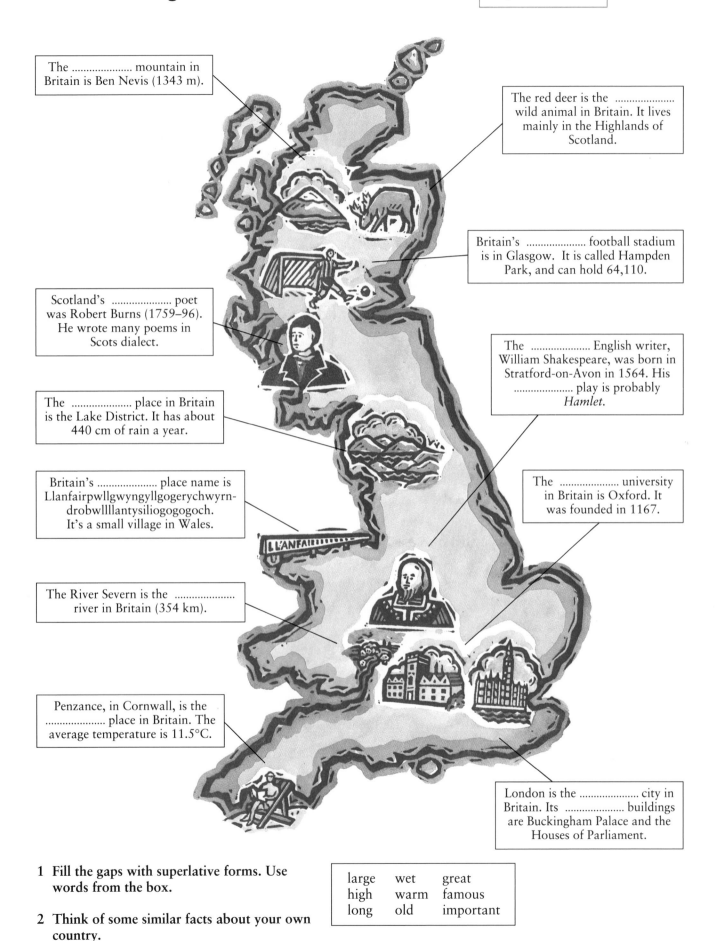

The .... mountain in Britain is Ben Nevis (1343 m).

The red deer is the .... wild animal in Britain. It lives mainly in the Highlands of Scotland.

Britain's .... football stadium is in Glasgow. It is called Hampden Park, and can hold 64,110.

Scotland's .... poet was Robert Burns (1759–96). He wrote many poems in Scots dialect.

The .... English writer, William Shakespeare, was born in Stratford-on-Avon in 1564. His .... play is probably *Hamlet*.

The .... place in Britain is the Lake District. It has about 440 cm of rain a year.

Britain's .... place name is Llanfairpwllgwyngyllgogerychwyrn-drobwllllantysiliogogogoch. It's a small village in Wales.

The .... university in Britain is Oxford. It was founded in 1167.

The River Severn is the .... river in Britain (354 km).

Penzance, in Cornwall, is the .... place in Britain. The average temperature is 11.5°C.

London is the .... city in Britain. Its .... buildings are Buckingham Palace and the Houses of Parliament.

1 **Fill the gaps with superlative forms. Use words from the box.**

2 **Think of some similar facts about your own country.**

large	wet	great
high	warm	famous
long	old	important

4 Yourself and others

1 **In the class**
   – who's the tallest?
   – who's the youngest?
   – who's got the largest family?
   – who speaks the most languages?
   – who's the fittest?
   – who's the most musical?

2 **Write a question of your own. Find out the answer.**

Grammar Checklist

Comparative & superlative adjectives

1-syllable (& some 2-syllable) adjs: + **-er, -est**
big, bigger, biggest
happy, happier, happiest
   (*not* more bigger, more happier)

2 or more syllables: **more, most** + *adj.*
helpful, **more** helpful, **most** helpful
attractive, **more** attractive, **most** attractive

Irregular forms:

good, **better, best**
bad, **worse, worst**
much, | **more, most**
many, |
little, **less, least**
far, **farther, farthest /**
   further, furthest

Comparative structures

adj. + **-er** | **than**
more + *adj.* |

Their house is | older | **than** ours.
            | **more** expensive |

Which is older, their house **or** ours?

Superlative structures

adj. + **-est** | ... (**in**) ...
most + *adj.* |

It's the | longest | river **in** Europe.
       | **most** beautiful |

Which is the longest river in Europe?
   (*not* Which is longest river ...)
   (*not* of Europe.)

See also Reference section, page 136.

Focus on Form

1 -er and -est

tall	hot	large	dry
cheap	thin	safe	funny
fast	wet	nice	happy

Add -er and -est to these adjectives.

Use three of them in sentences of your own.

2 Comparative adjectives

Examples:

A New York's a busy city, isn't it?
B Yes, but Tokyo's busier.
A I think dogs are very intelligent animals.
B Yes, but cats are more intelligent.

Have similar conversations. A thinks that

a Italy's a hot country
b English is a difficult language
c Manchester United are a good football team
d *Yesterday* is a beautiful song
e crocodiles are ugly
f cars are dangerous
g there are a lot of people in the USSR

3 ... than ...

Choose one thing from each box below, and ask your partner to compare them.

Examples:

woman – man
The man is older than the woman.
The woman's hair is longer than the man's.

telephone – chicken
Telephones are more useful than chickens.
Chickens are cheaper than telephones.

4 Superlatives

Do you agree with these opinions? If not, change them so that they are true for you.

> The weather forecast is the most interesting programme on TV.

> Farmers are the most important members of society.

> The safest way to travel is by bus.

> Chess is the most exciting game in the world.

> British cooking is the best in the world.

> The aeroplane is the greatest invention of all time.

5 Pronunciation

How do you say the words and phrases below?

a cleaner   quieter   livelier   funnier
   The people are friendlier.
   The atmosphere's quieter.

b She's younger than I am.
   Their office is bigger than mine.
   The film was more interesting than the book.

c largest   oldest   highest
   It's the highest mountain in the world.

🔲 **Now listen and check your answers.**

14 About town

1 Places to go

1 Imagine you've got some friends staying with you. During their stay they want to

– go shopping
– have an evening out
– go sightseeing
– get some exercise
– go somewhere after midnight
– go to your own favourite place in the town

Say where you would take them, and say something about each place.

2 Work in pairs.

Student A: You're spending a few days in B's home town. Think of a few particular things you would like to do (e.g. go out in a boat, eat some seafood, listen to some jazz).

Student B: Find out what A wants to do, and suggest some suitable places.

2 Can you tell me the way to …?

Destination 1: ....
Go out of the station and turn .... At
the end of the road, turn .... into
.... Street, go under the .... and
turn .... again at the .... It's
along there on your ....

Destination 2: ....
Go out of the station and turn ....
Carry on until you get to the ....
Turn .... and go straight on past the
.... till you get to the .... and
turn .... You'll see it on your
....

Destination 3: ....
Go out of the station and turn .... Go
through the .... and you'll come to
.... Street. Turn .... , and then
turn .... at the .... You'll see it
at the .... of the street.

1 You will hear three people giving
directions from the station. For each one

– find the destination
– fill the gaps in the text

Now choose one of the three destinations
and give directions back to the station.

2 **Work in pairs.**

Look at your own map in the back of the
book, and tell your partner where you want
to go. Follow his/her directions, and mark
the places on the map.

3 Home sweet home?

1 Which three of these adjectives describe
your home town best? Say why.

quiet	clean	friendly
busy	ugly	exciting
dirty	lively	beautiful
noisy	boring	interesting

2 Imagine you're visiting your town as a
tourist. You want to send home a postcard
saying what you think of the place.

– What view of the town will you choose?
– Write the postcard.

4 Los Angeles

READING

1 Here are some photographs of the Los Angeles area. Match them with the descriptions opposite.

2 **Which places would you recommend to someone who says**

   a 'Are there any good places to take the children?'

   b 'I'd love to know how they made all those Hollywood movies.'

   c 'I've never met a famous movie star face to face.'

   d 'I just want to relax and have a good time.'

3 **Imagine you are going to visit Los Angeles. You only have time to go to *two* places. Which would you choose?**

S pend a lazy afternoon down at **Malibu Lagoon**. Many of Hollywood's younger film stars and directors come here to relax, and some have homes here by the sea. You may see them jogging on the beach or shopping for yoghurt and diet drinks in the supermarkets. Malibu is also an excellent beach for surfing, and champion surfers come here from all over the world.

G o on a tour of the exclusive suburbs of **Beverly Hills** and **Belair**. Here you can see the homes of the rich and famous – magnificent houses built in every possible style, and surrounded by green lawns, swimming pools and high security fences. The streets here are spotlessly clean, and there are Rolls Royces everywhere you look.

H ave a look round **Universal Studios**, where some of Hollywood's greatest films were made. You can take a guided tour which will take you through the film sets and behind the scenes to the dressing rooms, and will bring you face to face with King Kong and the shark from Jaws.

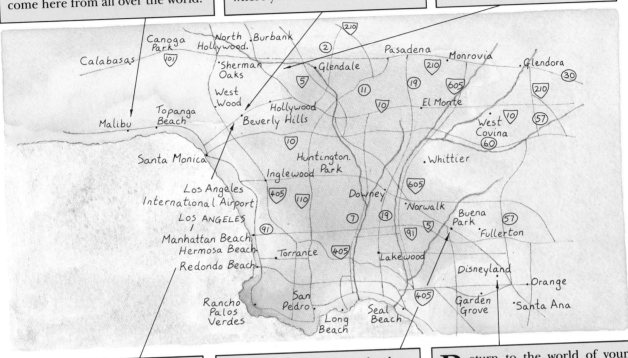

D rive down **Sunset Boulevard**, probably the most famous street in Los Angeles. Here you can see every side of the city's character – cheap nightclubs side by side with smart boutiques and expensive restaurants. At the western end of the Boulevard is the Beverly Hills Hotel, where visiting film stars, directors and writers go to sign their contracts.

I f you're tired of Disneyland, go and see the nearby **Movieland Wax Museum**, and admire the wax figures of famous stars such as Gary Cooper, Yul Brynner, the Marx Brothers and Brigitte Bardot – all in scenes from their best-known films. The museum also has a fascinating collection of the cameras used to make the very first moving pictures in the early days of cinema.

R eturn to the world of your childhood by spending a day at **Disneyland**, a place for children of all ages. At Disneyland you can go on a boat journey through a tropical jungle; you can take a train through the American Wild West; travel in a spaceship to the stars; take a trip on a monorail; plunge into a pool at Splash Mountain; … or just sit in the sun and eat ice cream.

LISTENING

🖭 **You will hear a woman talking about a holiday in the Los Angeles area.**

1 **Which of the six places did she visit? Where else did she go?**

2 **She uses these adjectives. Who or what is she talking about?**

scruffy	beautiful
expensive	polite and friendly
enormous	wonderful

Past and present

1 Changes

1 Here are some extracts from people's letters.
What has happened in between?

Last year

I've got a temporary job in London -
working for a company in the city. It
pays quite well, but it's a bit boring.
I'm still going out with Bob, of course.

What has happened?

The woman has left London. She's gone abroad.

....

Now

I'm in Italy, working in a hotel in
Rome - just a temporary job as a
receptionist - and I'm going out
with someone called Riccardo, who
I met at a party. He's really nice.

Last year

The doctor says I'm ten kilos overweight
and that unless I give up smoking
immediately I'm heading for a heart
attack. Well, I'm sure he's right.

What has happened?

....

Now

Three months now without a cigarette.
I still miss it, of course, especially
after meals, but I do feel a lot
healthier. I go jogging every day, and
I'm down to 75 kilos already.

2 What changes have there been in your life in the last five years?
Write five things that you have done.

2 What has happened?

Positive & negative sentences • not ... yet

She's not in hospital any more.	She's left hospital.
He's still asleep.	He hasn't woken up yet.
They're still having lunch.	They haven't finished yet.

1 Say what these people have or haven't done.

a She's still reading *War and Peace*.
b He's still living at home.
c They haven't got their car any more.
d She's still in bed.
e They're living in Kenya now.
f She can't find her passport.

2 How could you answer these questions?

a Are they still in Berlin?
b Is it still raining?
c Is he still going out with Martina?
d Are you still learning Russian?
e Is there any cheese left?
f Where's Charlie?

3 Headline news

Imagine you see this article in today's paper.

1 Look at the headline and the photos. What do you think has happened?

2 Read the article and make up an ending to the story.

3 Listen to the news item. How did the story really end?

POLICE HUNT FOR CHILDREN
Helicopters and dogs join search

Sally Baird

Robert Lawson

Jean Lawson

POLICE are searching for four children who have been missing from their home near Glasgow for nearly 24 hours.

The three five-year-old girls and a boy of three were last seen early yesterday afternoon by a neighbour. No-one has seen them since.

Police have organised a search of the neighbourhood to try to find the four children. As well as 100 police, the team includes two helicopters, trained dogs, divers and 200 volunteers.

Inspector Peter Douglas, who is leading the search, said last night "We can think of no reason why the children have gone missing. We have looked everywhere, and now we are looking again."

Parents' plea

The parents of the missing children last night spoke on TV news about their ordeal

A police officer searches houses for the four children who have been missing overnight.

4 Experiences

1 Complete these questions.

Have you ever ……………?

Have you ever ……………?

Have you ever ……………?

Only once. I didn't like it much.

No, I haven't. I don't eat meat.

Yes, I have, but only as a passenger.

No, I haven't. I think they're dangerous.

No, but I'd love to go there.

Yes, I often go there on business.

2 Ask and answer these questions. Then add two questions of your own.

Have you ever written a poem?

Have you ever been to a casino?

Have you ever seen a play by Shakespeare?

Have you ever drunk *sake*?

Have you ever been sailing?

Have you ever acted in a play?

Grammar Checklist

Past participles

Regular verbs: add -ed or -d
(same as past tense)

play – play**ed**; arrive – arriv**ed**

Irregular verbs: see list on page 143.

Present perfect tense

have/has (**not**) + *past participle*
(*Short forms:* 've, 's, haven't, hasn't)

I've **stopped** smoking.
The President **has** arrived. (*not* … ~~is arrived~~.)
I **haven't found** a job.

still & yet

He **hasn't** woken up **yet**. (= He's **still** asleep.)
Have you finished that book **yet**?
    (= Are you **still** reading it?)

Questions

have/has + *subject* + *past participle*
Have you **found** a job?
    (Yes, I **have**. / No, I **haven't**.)
Has he **arrived**?
Where **have** you **been**?

ever & never

Position: just before the past participle

Have you **ever** ridden a motorbike?
    (*not* ~~Did you ever ride~~ …)
He's **never** been to the USA.

See also Reference section, page 137.

Focus on Form

1 Past participle forms

Write the past participles of these verbs.

Infinitive	Past	Past participle
finish	finished	....
write	wrote	....
break	broke	....
ring	rang	....
drink	drank	....
have	had	....
lose	lost	....
put	put	....

Use three of the verbs in sentences of your own, using the Present perfect tense.

2 Statements

Look at the pictures. What do you think has happened?

Example: *Picture 1*

He's lost his mother.
Someone's taken his ball.
He's fallen over and hurt his leg.

3 Negatives

Examples:

A Suki Yaki's delicious, isn't it?
B I don't know. I've never eaten it.
A Rio's a lovely city, isn't it?
B I don't know. I haven't been there.

Have similar conversations. Talk about

a Tibet	e *The New York Times*
b basketball	f Turkish coffee
c caviare	g *The Magnificent Seven*
d The Hilton	

4 Questions

Think of three things you think your partner has done today, and three things you think he/she hasn't done. Write them down. Examples:

You've driven a car today.
You've drunk some coffee.
You haven't had lunch.
You haven't written any letters.

Now find out if you were right by asking questions. Examples:

A Have you driven a car today?
B Yes, I have.
A Have you had lunch?
B No, I haven't.

5 Pronunciation

How do you say the words and phrases below?

a written   forgotten   broken
   I've written a poem.
   done   gone
   They've gone to the cinema.

b I haven't seen her.
   He hasn't found it.

c Have you ever worked in an office?
   Has she ever been to Hong Kong?

d Are you still reading that book?
   We're still living in the same flat.

🔲 **Now listen and check your answers.**

16 Free time

1 Leisure activities

Louisa   Age 10   School pupil

Carsten   Age 20   Musician

Patrick   Age 39   Radio producer

Josephine   Age 75   Retired teacher

1 **What do you think**

  – Louisa   – Patrick
  – Carsten – Josephine

do in their free time? Make sentences using expressions from the box.

🖭 Now listen to them talking about their leisure activities. Were you right? What other activities do they mention?

2 Find out how your partner spends his/her free time. Make notes. Write a paragraph from your notes.

swimming	jazz
theatre	cycling
cooking	guitar
languages	running
collecting shells	golf
knitting	walking
reading	piano

2 Spectator sports

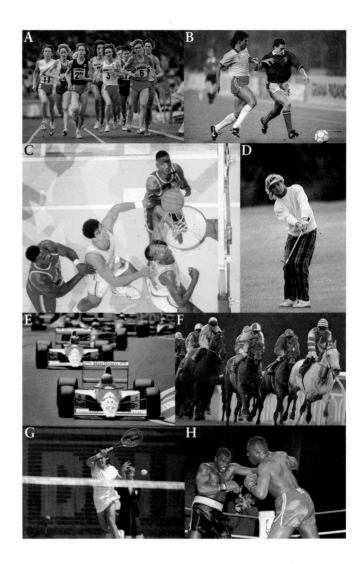

1 Look at the photographs.

  a **What sports can you see?**

  b **Talk about the sports that use a ball. Use words from the box.**

kick	hole	net
throw	goal	club
hit	basket	racquet

  c **Look at these remarks. Which sports could they be about?**

> The referee has blown his whistle.

> It's going to be a close race.

> They've scored again.

> It was a tremendous match.

2 **Which of the sports do you watch? Have you ever done any of them yourself?**

3 Would you enjoy ...?

1 **Read about the person in the box. Would he enjoy these activities? Why? Why not?**
  a parachute jumping
  b bird watching
  c water skiing
  d horse riding
  e stamp collecting
  f playing in a band

2 **Which activity do you think you would enjoy most? Which would you enjoy least?**

He's quite fit.

He enjoys being in the open air.

He likes going fast.

He doesn't like being in crowded places.

He doesn't like animals.

He can play the guitar.

He's a good swimmer.

He's afraid of heights.

He hasn't got much patience.

4 Board games round the world

READING

Work in pairs. Look at these three board games. Choose one game and try playing it.

Game 1: Pong Hau K'i
This game for two players comes from China. It is also played in Korea.
The board consists of five points joined by lines, like this:

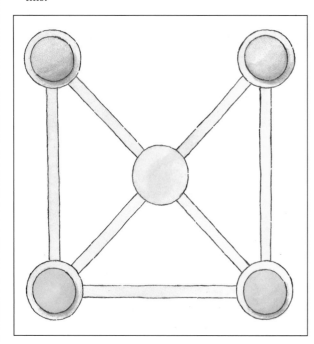

Each player has two stones of the same colour, which are placed as shown at the start of the game. Either blue or red can start.
Players take it in turns to move one stone along a line to an empty point. A player can only move one stone one place during a turn.
The aim of the game is to block the other player's pieces so that they can't move.

Game 2: Achi
This two-player game is a variant of *Noughts and Crosses*. It comes from Ghana.
The board consists of nine points joined by horizontal, vertical and diagonal lines:

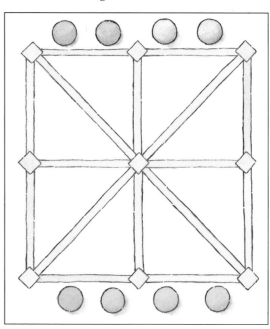

Each player has four stones.
Players take it in turns to place their stones on empty points on the board, until all eight stones have been placed. So far the game is just like *Noughts and Crosses*: if a player makes a line of three (in any direction) he or she wins the game.
If not, players continue by moving a piece along a line to an empty point until one player gets three stones in a line, and wins.

Game 3: Tchuka Ruma

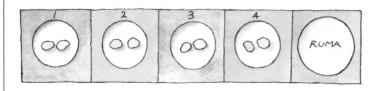

This is an East Indian game for one player. It is played on a board which has four small holes and one larger hole, which is called the Ruma. At the start of the game, each of the small holes has two stones in it.
You must lift the stones from any hole and 'sow' them from left to right, dropping one in each hole as you pass. For example, suppose you choose hole 1 to begin with:

Start:	2	2	2	2	0
After move:	0	3	3	2	0

You now lift the stones from the hole in which you finished and 'sow' these again from left to right.
If the last stone falls into an empty hole, you lose. If not, you sow again starting from the hole in which you finished. If the last stone falls in the Ruma, you can choose any hole to begin your next move.
If you reach the Ruma with more than one stone in hand, you continue sowing at hole 1.
The aim is to get all the stones into the Ruma.

LISTENING

1 This game is called the Snake Game.
   How do you think it is played?

2 🖭 You will hear someone talking about
   the game. Listen and answer the questions.

   a How old is the game?
   Where does it come from?

   b Complete these sentences:

   The aim of the game is ......

   Each player has ......

   To play the game:

   – One player ......
   – The other player ......
   – If the player ...... he/she ......
   – The player who ...... wins the game.

Adapted from *Board Games Round the World*,
by Robbie Bell and Michael Cornelius.

17 Obligation

1 Do you have to …?

must(n't) & (don't) have to • can & can't

1 Make true sentences about your school from the table.

You	must/have to don't have to can mustn't/can't	pay for classes. arrive late. do homework. buy your own books. eat in class. wear a uniform. speak English.

2 Where would you expect to see these signs?
Say what they mean using verbs from the table above.

A

B SILENCE

C **POSTAGE PAID**
No stamp needed

D P

E

F ✗ ✓

G AMERICAN EXPRESS Cards Welcome

H **ADULTS $5.00 CHILDREN $3.00** *Children under 5 free*

I

3 Work in pairs. Choose one of these places, and write a 'rule' for it.
Then pass your paper to another pair to continue.

a cinema	a restaurant	a bus
a swimming pool	a nightclub	a hotel
a football stadium	a hospital	a beach

2 House rules

1 You're thinking of renting a room in someone's house. What questions might you ask the owner using *Can I ... ?* and *Do I have to ... ?*

Can I keep pets?

Do I have to share a room?

2 Work in pairs.

Student A: You want to rent a room. Find out about the house rules from the owner.

Student B: You're the owner of the house. Answer A's questions.

3 Military service

 You will hear an interview with a Dutch soldier who is doing his military service.

1 Look at the questions in the box. Which questions does he answer?

> a Does everyone have to do military service?
> b At what age do you have to do it?
> c How long does it last?
> d Is it very hard work?
> e Can you choose the kind of work you want to do?
> f Do you use weapons?
> g How much leave do you get?
> h Do you think it's a useful experience?
> i Do most people enjoy it?

2 Do you have to do military service in your country? What differences are there?

4 Personal problems

My son steals

We're an ordinary married couple with two children, an 11-year-old boy and a 4-year-old girl. Two years ago, my son started to steal from me. If I catch him, he cries a lot and promises never to do it again. I don't think he's unhappy: we get on well as a family, and we all do things together in the evenings and at weekends. We give him plenty of pocket money, too. I just can't understand why he keeps on stealing.

> She ought not to give him any more pocket money.

> She should punish him every time he steals from her.

> She shouldn't leave money lying around the house.

> She ought to ask the boy's doctor for help.

> She shouldn't punish him – she should try to find out why he steals.

1 **Do you agree with any of the advice in the bubbles?**

2 Now choose one of these problems, and say what you think the person should do.

Will she pay?

Last year, my girlfriend wanted to take a business course but she didn't have enough money. Her parents couldn't help, so I lent her the money. Now she's finished the course, and has found a good job, but she hasn't offered to pay me back any of the money. I've mentioned it once or twice, but she just laughs and talks about something else. I love my girlfriend, but I want my money back too.

She doesn't like me

I've got a good job in an office, which I really enjoy. Recently, we got a new manager, and for some reason she doesn't like me. I've tried to be friendly to her, but she just criticises me all the time. I've got good qualifications, and I work hard, and I could easily find another job somewhere else. But I'd rather stay where I am.

A psychologist's replies are on page 123.

Grammar Checklist

Modal verbs

must/mustn't
can/can't   + *infinitive* <u>without</u> to
should/shouldn't

You **mustn't** shout. (*not* … ~~mustn't to~~ …)
We **can** go now.
You **should** speak to him.

must & have to

must *and* **have to** *mean almost the same.*

You **must** take your shoes off.
He **has to** wear a suit.

mustn't & don't have to

You **mustn't** = don't do this
You **mustn't** talk in here. (= don't talk)

You **don't have to** = it's not necessary
He **doesn't have to** wear a suit. (*but he can if he wants to*)

can & can't

He **can** go home at weekends.
You **can't** smoke here. (= you mustn't smoke)

Questions about obligation

Can I smoke?
Do I have to wear a suit?

should(n't) & ought (not) to

should(n't) + *infinitive*
ought (not) + to + *infinitive*

| They | should ought to | spend more time together. |

| You | shouldn't ought not to | work so hard. |

See also Reference section, page 138.

Focus on Form

1 Mustn't & don't have to

You're the manager of a company, and you're telling a new employee some of the rules. Make sentences with *mustn't* or *don't have to*.

Examples:

wear a suit
You don't have to wear a suit.

listen to music
You mustn't listen to music.

a smoke in the office
b work on Saturdays
c make private phone calls
d wear shorts
e pay for your coffee
f stay after 4 o'clock
g use the Directors' car park
h type your own letters

2 Question forms

You're the new employee. Ask questions with *Can I...?* and *Do I have to...?*

Examples:

Do I have to wear a suit?
Can I listen to music?

3 Different words – same meaning

Student A: Make a sentence from Table 1.

Student B: Make a sentence from Table 2 that means the same as A's sentence.

Examples:

A You have to cook it.
B You mustn't eat it raw.

A You don't have to cook it.
B You can eat it raw.

4 Should(n't) & ought (not) to

Reply to the remarks below with two pieces of advice, one positive and one negative. Use *should*, *shouldn't*, *ought to* and *ought not to*.

Examples:

I'm so tired these days.
You ought to take a holiday.
You shouldn't go to bed so late.

I find it very difficult to make friends.
You should smile more often.
You ought not to be so rude to people.

a I've got a terrible cough.
b I never seem to have enough money.
c My children never do what I say.
d I can never get to sleep at night.
e I find evenings at home so boring!

5 Pronunciation

How do you say the words and phrases below?

a You must buy your own books.
You should see a doctor.
You can stay here.

b mustn't   shouldn't   can't
You mustn't talk.
You shouldn't drink coffee.
You can't smoke in here.

c have to   ought to
Do I have to speak English?
You ought to take a holiday.

▭ **Now listen and check your answers.**

Table 1

You	have to / must	stay here. / get up. / be quiet. / give it back. / take your shoes off. / come back early
	don't have to	cook it. / do it now. / deliver it yourself.

Table 2

You	can	eat it raw. / keep them on. / post it. / go out. / leave it till later.
	can't / mustn't	make a noise. / stay in bed. / keep it. / come back late.

18 A day's work

1 Occupations

1 What are the occupations of the people in the picture?

2 Look at the bubbles below. Who are the speakers?

3 Choose an occupation. Write two or three sentences about where you work and what you do. Other students will guess who you are.

A

I work in a hotel ... I sit at the desk by the entrance ... I deal with enquiries and reservations ... Guests leave their keys with me when they go out.

B

I work for a large company ... I have my own office and a secretary ... I look after the company's money ... Once a year I calculate the company's profits ... It's a very well paid job.

C

I work for a radio station ... I spend most of the time in a studio ... I play records and tell jokes ... Sometimes I work till one or two in the morning.

D

I'm self-employed ... I work in other people's houses ... I put pipes and taps in their kitchens and bathrooms ... People often call me out in emergencies.

E

I spend most of the day at home ... I take the children to school, do the housework, do the shopping and cook meals.

2 Job satisfaction

1 Choose one of the occupations in the picture (or your own occupation). How might you answer these questions?

- How much do you earn?
- Do you have to work hard?
- Do you get long holidays?

- Do you enjoy your job?
- What are the good things about it?
- What are the bad things?

2 Interview each other. Ask and answer the questions.

3 A working life

1 Put the events in this woman's career in a
more sensible order.

	She got the sack.
	She became a researcher for a TV programme.
	She was promoted to accounts manager.
	She applied for a lot of jobs.
	She studied economics at university.
	She became a TV presenter.
	She left her job.
	She worked in a restaurant.
	She got a job in a department store.

2 🔲 Listen to the woman talking
and check your answers.

Listen again. What does she say
about these things?

– why she left her job
– why she got the sack
– how she got into television

4 Applying for a job

READING

1 Look at the advertisement.
  What do you think the job might involve?
  What kind of person would be suitable?

**Receptionist/
General assistant**

for busy 3 star hotel in Jersey.
Applicants must be mature and out-
going, with a minimum of one year's
experience. An excellent salary, a
uniform and your own bedroom will
be provided.
Please supply a recent photograph
and C.V. to:
**Alan Chalmers
Trinity Hotel, Jersey
Tel: 0534 199388**

Ferns Hotel
6 Arundel Place
Brighton
England

14 January 19

Dear Mr Chalmers,

I am writing to apply for the job of
Receptionist/General Assistant, which you
advertised recently in Hotel & Catering
Magazine.

I am 25 years old. I have 5 'O' level
passes, including French and Mathematics. I
also have the Pitman Secretarial Diploma. Since
leaving college I have had several years'
experience doing secretarial and general office
work in London, including several months as
receptionist for a large company.

At the moment I am working as a receptionist
at the Ferns Hotel, a small private hotel in
Brighton. I have been employed there for the
past six months.

I am interested in working as a receptionist
in your hotel as I enjoy hotel work and now I
would like to broaden my experience.

I enclose a photograph and a full curriculum
vitae, and I would be happy to send any further
details you may require.

Yours sincerely

Penny Wright.

Penny Wright

2 Read Penny Wright's letter of
  application.
  How suitable do you think she is
  for the job?

READING AND LISTENING

1 Here is some advice about how to do well in job interviews. Do you think it is all good advice? Would you add anything else?

2  You will hear four parts of Penny Wright's interview for the job in the hotel.

How well did she do?
Make notes below.

Before the interview

Find out – everything you can about the firm. If you're interested in them, they'll be more interested in you.

Think – about the job. What qualities does it require? And what makes you the right person to get it?

Be prepared – to talk about yourself: your qualifications, your qualities, your interests. You'll probably be nervous during the interview, so think about what you'll say beforehand.

The interview itself

Be early – If you're late, the interviewer will think you're not very interested. People who arrive late for interviews arrive late for work too. So allow for heavy traffic, and getting lost.

Wear – reasonable clothes. Be comfortable, but smart.

Be polite – as you would when you meet any stranger.

Listen – What is the interviewer asking you? What does he/she want to know? If you don't understand the question, say so!

Talk – clearly, at your usual speed. Don't mumble.

Answer – Don't always use just 'yes' or 'no'. Try to get a conversation going.

Look – the interviewer in the eye. Don't look down at your shoes or out of the window.

Be honest – If you don't know the answer to a question, don't be afraid to say so. If you lie, the interviewer will probably catch you out.

Sell yourself – The interview is a chance to advertise yourself, so get your good points across.

Ask – questions yourself. About the job; about pay and conditions; about when they will decide.

At the end of the interview, say thank you and leave; don't hang about.

Afterwards...

Try to decide how well you did. Think about what you were asked and how you responded – it's one way of learning for yourself about coping with interviews.

Did you prepare?

_____

_____

_____

How did you do?

_____

_____

_____

_____

_____

_____

_____

_____

_____

_____

1

There's a new arrival at the place where you work or study. Tell him or her some of the rules.

2

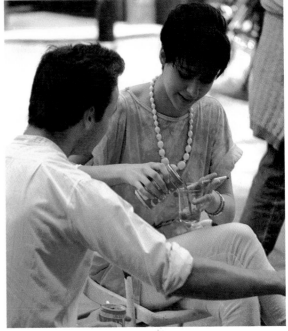

You're talking to a friend from another town, and discussing whose town is better to live in. Make three comparisons.

3

You're going for an interview for a job as a tourist guide. Think of three questions they might ask you, and three questions you might ask them.

4

Talk about one of these topics. Can you keep talking for one minute?

world records

hotels

a good job

today's news

something I've never done

the best spots in town

problem pages

indoor games

outdoor games

5 How are things?

Imagine you have just received this letter from an old friend. Write a suitable reply.

especially as I've never been there before.

How are things with you? Are you still working in that cafe or have you got a proper job now? And have you found a new flat yet? Do write and tell me all your news.

By the way, I'll be in your part of the world next month (16th – 25th). Why don't we try and meet? It would be great to see you again after all this time.

Love to you and the family,

Jo

6 Careers advice

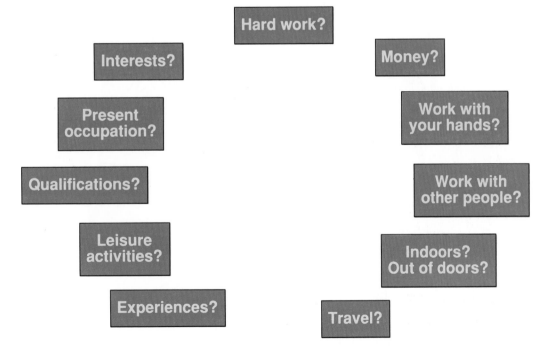

Hard work?

Interests?

Money?

Present occupation?

Work with your hands?

Qualifications?

Work with other people?

Leisure activities?

Indoors? Out of doors?

Experiences?

Travel?

Student A

You are not sure what career would be best for you, so you go to the Careers Advice Centre for an interview. Answer their questions.

Students B, C and D

You work at the Careers Advice Centre. Interview Student A, and advise him/her what career to take up.

1 How did it happen?

Past continuous tense • Past simple tense

1 📼 You will hear three people talking about accidents they have had.

Find the people in the picture.
What happened to them?
What were they doing at the time?

2 Talk about other people in the picture. What happened to them? What were they doing at the time? Use the verbs in the box to help you.

bite	hit
break	hurt
cut	tear
fall	trip

Example:

She was walking beside a river. She tripped and fell into the water.

2 Joining ideas

when & while

1 These sentences make four different stories. Which sentences go together?
   Tell each story using *when* or *while*.

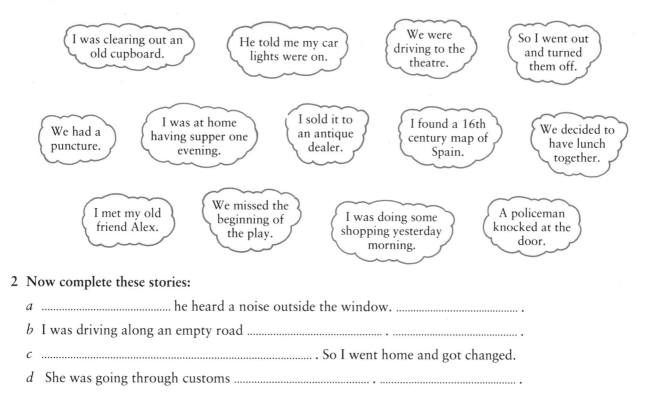

I was clearing out an old cupboard.

He told me my car lights were on.

We were driving to the theatre.

So I went out and turned them off.

We had a puncture.

I was at home having supper one evening.

I sold it to an antique dealer.

I found a 16th century map of Spain.

We decided to have lunch together.

I met my old friend Alex.

We missed the beginning of the play.

I was doing some shopping yesterday morning.

A policeman knocked at the door.

2 Now complete these stories:

a .... he heard a noise outside the window. ....

b I was driving along an empty road ....

c .... So I went home and got changed.

d She was going through customs ....

3 Mystery flight

1 On 13th July 1989, Thomas
   Root, a Washington lawyer,
   took off in his light aircraft on a
   routine business trip. You will
   read a newspaper story about
   what happened.

   Student A: Turn to page 121 and
   read the first part of the story.

   Student B: Turn to page 122 and
   read the second part of the story.

2 Work in pairs.

   Retell your part of the story.
   What happened at points A, B, C
   and D on the map?

   Can you think of an explanation
   for what happened?

Washington lawyer in flight mystery

4 Setting a scene

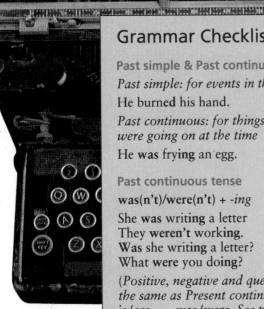

Through the rain, I saw a lighted window and a sign which said "Sam's Place". I went in and sat down. I looked around me.

An old man with grey hair was _____ at the piano, _____ a dance tune. In the centre of the room, in a space between the tables, a man and a woman were _____ cheek to cheek.

There was a young couple _____ hands in the corner, _____ together in low voices. At another table, a group of six men were _____ cards.

At a table by the door, there was a young woman _____ alone, _____ nervously around her.

The only other customer was a tall man in a white suit. He was _____ at the bar, _____ a large cigar and _____ the dancers intently.

I walked over to the bar and ordered a drink.

1 Fill the gaps with words from the box.

smoking	sitting
dancing	watching
standing	talking
holding	playing
looking	

2 Write another scene for the story. Begin with one of the following:

It was midnight when I got back to the hotel. I went into the lobby to get my key.

The apartment wasn't locked. I opened the door slowly, and went inside.

It was nearly 5 o'clock. I pulled back a curtain and looked down into the street.

Grammar Checklist

Past simple & Past continuous

Past simple: for events in the past
He burned his hand.

Past continuous: for things that were going on at the time
He **was** frying an egg.

Past continuous tense

was(n't)/were(n't) + *-ing*

She **was** writing a letter
They **weren't** working.
Was she writing a letter?
What **were** you doing?

(*Positive, negative and question forms are the same as Present continuous, but* **is/are** → **was/were**. *See page 26.*)

when & while

Past continuous + **when** *+ past simple*
He **was** frying an egg **when** he burned his hand.

Past simple + **while/when** *+ past continuous*
He burned his hand **while** he **was** frying an egg.

-ing forms

There was a woman selling oranges.
   (= There was a woman[. She was] selling oranges.)

He was sitting in a corner, reading a book.
   (= He was sitting in a corner [and he was] reading a book.)

See also Reference section, page 139.

Focus on Form

1 Positive & negative

Example:

I (feel) very hungry ...

A I was feeling very hungry ...
B ... so I bought a bar of chocolate.

A I wasn't feeling very hungry ...
B ... so I just ordered a salad.

Student A: Make a positive or negative sentence.

Student B: Choose a suitable ending from the box.

a I (feel) very hungry ...
b She (work) very hard ...
c We (get on) well together ...
d It (rain) ...
e I (wear) a jacket and tie ...
f They (use) their spare room ...

> ... so we went for a walk.
> ... so I just ordered a salad.
> ... so I used it as a study.
> ... so I decided to leave.
> ... so I bought a bar of chocolate.
> ... so they wouldn't let me into the restaurant.
> ... so I slept in the sitting room.
> ... so they gave her the sack.
> ... so I suggested meeting again at the weekend.
> ... so I felt rather hot.
> ... so I took my umbrella.
> ... so I didn't disturb her.

2 Asking questions

Example:

I remember him well. He was wearing ...... and he was carrying ...... enormous suitcases.

A What was he wearing?
B (He was wearing) sunglasses.

A How many suitcases was he carrying?
B (He was carrying) three.

Ask (and answer) questions about these texts:

John and I first met 5 years ago. I was living in ... (1) at the time. I was studying ...(2) at university, and in the evenings I was ...(3) to make more money. John was working in ...(4), and was earning about ...(5) a month.

My friend Jane came to see us last night. I didn't hear her knock at the door, because I was ...(6) at the time. My parents didn't hear her either, because they were ...(7) in the back garden. Eventually, I saw her through the window. She was sitting ...(8), writing ...(9).

3 -ing forms

You are helping the police look for a man. The pictures show the occasions when you think you saw him.

Look at the pictures for 30 seconds, and then cover the page. Try to remember where he was and what he was doing.

Example:

I saw him in the library. He was wearing sunglasses, and he was sitting at a table reading a magazine.

4 Pronunciation

How do you say the words and phrases below?

a I was wearing a jacket.
   I wasn't looking.

b They were dancing.
   They weren't feeling hungry.

c What was he doing?
   Was he carrying a suitcase?

d There were three people waiting.
   There was a newspaper on the table.

🔲 Now listen and check your answers.

1 Familiar faces

1 The people below were all world leaders.
How many of them can you recognise?

🎙️ Listen to the tape. Who are the two
speakers describing?

2 Try to remember exactly what some of
the other people look(ed) like. Use the
words in the box to help you.

dark	thin	long	straight	bald
fair	thick	short	wavy	moustache
large	fat	tall	curly	beard

2 How old?

1 How old do you think these people are?
  Make sentences from the table.

	(about) 35 (years old).		
He's	in	his	teens.
			twenties.
She's		her	thirties.
			...

2 Work in pairs. Find out if your partner has
  the same people as you. Talk about ages and
  physical features.

  Student A: Look only at the people on page 121.

  Student B: Look only at the people on page 122.

A I've been teaching for 25 years now.

B I think I'm getting a bit old to have a baby now.

C I was just a baby during the Second World War.

D Only one more year at university and you'll have to start looking for a job.

E I'm buying him a razor for his birthday – he's just started shaving.

F She was born in 1915.

G I'm really looking forward to retiring next year.

3 Character sketch

1 The adjectives in the box are used to
  describe people's characters.

  Which of them do you think are good?
  Which do you think are bad?

  Which *three* adjectives describe you best?
  Tell your partner.

shy	generous
selfish	forgetful
friendly	self-confident
mean	bad-tempered
honest	easy-going
lazy	hard-working

2 🔲 You will hear three short scenes.

  What happens in each one?

  **What can you tell about the people's
  characters?**

3 Work in pairs. Choose a character adjective,
  and prepare a short scene of your own.

4 The Dream Game

Here's a psychological test which will reveal your innermost secrets.

LISTENING

1 🎧 On the tape, someone will ask you some questions. Make notes of your answers on a piece of paper.

2 In pairs, read the key opposite. What can you tell from your partner's answers? What can you tell about yourself?

READING

Here are the answers that two people gave for the Dream Game. How do you interpret them?

DISCUSSION

What do you think of the Dream Game? Do you agree with any of these statements?

a It's a useful and serious psychological test.
b I'm not sure if I take it seriously or not.
c It's fun but it's only a game.
d It's nonsense.

Kate, age 38

The house: It's a tiny cottage in the middle of the country, far away from any other house. It's very pretty, with a thatched roof, with flowers growing round the doorway.

The cup: It's a very big old china cup, very big, with warm milk in it.

The building: It's an old wooden shed, and it looks as if it's falling down. It's very very old, and dirty.

The garden: The garden is full of roses, and they're all different colours – red, pink, yellow, white, absolutely beautiful.

The wall: I'm not sure what to do, but I want to see what's on the other side, so I go through.

The water: Do I want to swim in it? Oh no, definitely not. It's horrible. It's green and muddy and slimy. I don't want to go anywhere near it.

Dennis, age 26

The house: It's a big, big, rambling old house, with a long drive going up to it. Lots of grounds around it, with different sorts of gardens. It's got lots of rooms, and a great big wide staircase.

The cup: It's a tiny, really fine bone china cup, and it's got what looks like liquid gold in the bottom of it.

The building: It's a little stone cottage, it's grey stone, and it's very small, and there's some smoke coming out of the chimney.

The garden: Well, it needs a lot of work. Everything's neglected and overgrown. Very tall flowers, and very long grass.

The wall: Yes, of course I go through it.

The water: It's a huge kind of lake, and the water's dark and calm, and there are fish in it. It's cold to swim in, but good too.

What your answers mean ...

Use this key to analyse your answers.

The House
The house is your idea of yourself.
The number of bedrooms is the number of people you want in your life.
If it is light inside, you probably have an optimistic nature.
An older house shows that you have a respect for tradition.

The cup
The cup is your idea of love.
Anything inside the cup shows what your experience of love has been so far in your life.

The building
This represents your idea of God.

The garden
This is your idea of creation, the world; or perhaps your country.

The wall
The wall is death. Do you go through the little door? Most people do, but some don't want to. Others look first.
The water is your idea of what happens after death.

Prediction

1 What will it be like?

will, won't & might

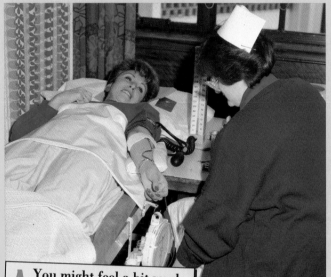

So you're planning to give blood?

Every week thousands of people give blood. If you've done it, you know how easy it is. If you're thinking about it – Dr Karen Hall has the answers to your questions.

1 Look at the questions. Can you answer them?

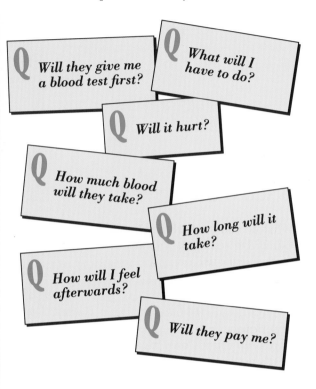

Q Will they give me a blood test first?

Q What will I have to do?

Q Will it hurt?

Q How much blood will they take?

Q How long will it take?

Q How will I feel afterwards?

Q Will they pay me?

Now look at the answers. Which questions do they go with?

A You might feel a bit weak, so you may want to rest for a while after giving blood. But you'll be back to normal in 4–6 hours.

A No, not in Britain, although in some countries they do pay for blood. You'll probably get a cup of tea and a biscuit.

A Just lie down and relax. The nurse will attach a needle to your arm, and the blood will flow down into a bag beside your bed. You don't have to do anything at all.

A No. It might hurt very slightly when the needle goes in, but after that you won't feel anything.

A About half a litre. But remember that you've got 5 litres of blood in your body, so it won't make much difference.

A Not long – about half an hour altogether.

A Yes. Before you give blood they need to find out which blood group you belong to. So the nurse will take a small sample of blood from the end of your finger.

2 Imagine that a friend is about to do one of these things for the first time:

    – go through customs   – go for a job interview
    – have a tooth filled   – travel by plane

Tell your friend what to expect. Say what you think *will* happen, *won't* happen and *might* happen.

2 If ...

Don't worry.

It won't attack

if

unless

we swim slowly towards it.

you don't panic.

it smells blood.

you keep calm.

it's very hungry.

1 Make sentences from the bubbles.

2 Continue these sentences using *if* or *unless*.
  a Don't worry. The dog won't bite ...
  b That meat'll go bad ...
  c We'll probably catch the train ...
  d They won't let you cross the border ...
  e She won't make any new friends ...
  f You'll ruin your eyesight ...

3 In the next few days

1 Choose any of the topics that interest you and make predictions.

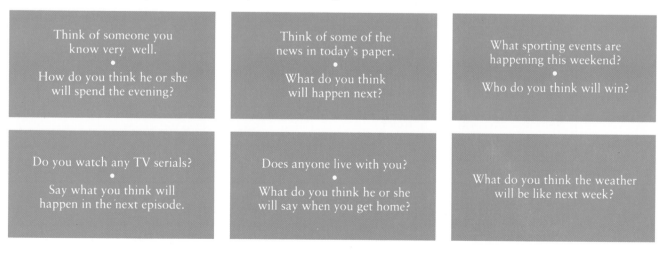

Think of someone you
know very well.
•
How do you think he or she
will spend the evening?

Think of some of the
news in today's paper.
•
What do you think
will happen next?

What sporting events are
happening this weekend?
•
Who do you think will win?

Do you watch any TV serials?
•
Say what you think will
happen in the next episode.

Does anyone live with you?
•
What do you think he or she
will say when you get home?

What do you think the weather
will be like next week?

2 Write down three of your predictions and see if they come true.

4 What's going to happen?

going to

1 ▭ Listen to the tape. Which pictures is the speaker talking about? Do you agree with him?

2 Look at the other pictures. What do you think is going to happen?

Grammar Checklist

will, won't & might

He**'ll** tell you what to do. (= He will ...)
They **won't** win the match.
   (= They will not ...)
She **might** see you later. (= Perhaps she will ...)
   (*not* ... ~~might to see~~ ...)

probably

Position: after **will**, *before* **won't**

They**'ll probably** win.
They **probably won't** win.

Questions with 'will'

will + *subject* + *infinitive*

Will they win the match?
When **will** she arrive?
   (*not* ~~When she will~~ ...)

if & unless

If/Unless + *Present simple*, ... **will/might** ...

If they **play** well, they**'ll** win.
   (*not* ... ~~will play~~ ...)

Unless we **leave** soon, │
If we **don't leave** soon, │ we'll miss the bus.

going to

Use **going to** *for things that have already started to happen.*

Oh dear – I think I'm **going to** cry. (I can feel the tears coming into my eyes.)
They're **going to** win. (They're 3–0 ahead, and there are only 3 minutes left.)
(For other uses of **going to** *see Unit 11.)*

See also Reference section, page 140.

Focus on Form

1 Will, won't & might

Do you think you'll sleep well tonight? Make a prediction from the table.

I	'll (probably) might (probably) won't	sleep well.

Are these predictions true for you? If necessary, change them to give your own opinion.

a I'll get married next year.
b It'll rain tomorrow.
c I'll have to go to the bank before the weekend.
d We'll finish this unit today.
e I'll have chips for dinner tonight.
f There'll be a new government before the end of the year.
g I'll go abroad before the end of the year.

2 Questions with will

Student A: A fortune teller is telling your fortune. Find out more by asking questions.

Student B: You are the fortune teller. Answer A's questions.

Example:
A Who will I meet?
B ....

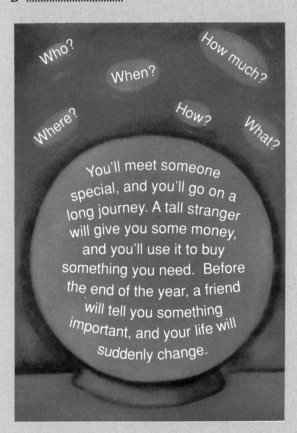

3 If & unless

Example: you complain to the manager ...
A If you complain to the manager ...
B ... I'm sure she'll give you your money back.
A Unless you complain to the manager ...
B ... you'll always get bad service.

Student A: Start a sentence with *If* or *Unless*.

Student B: Choose a suitable ending from the box.

a you complain to the manager ...
b I win the national lottery ...
c he arrives soon ...
d you write him a letter ...
e she retires soon ...
f you leave immediately ...

> ... we'll all have dinner together.
> ... I'll have to borrow some money from you.
> ... you'll always get bad service.
> ... it'll cheer him up.
> ... I'm sure she'll give you your money back.
> ... she'll make herself ill.
> ... he won't know our address.
> ... you might get there in time.
> ... I'll give a huge party.
> ... we'll have to go without him.
> ... I'll call the police.
> ... I'll apply for her job.

4 Pronunciation

How do you say the words and phrases below?

a I'll you'll he'll we'll they'll it'll
   He'll arrive soon.
   It'll rain tomorrow.

b What do you think she'll say?
   Where do you think they'll go?

c I'll probably go abroad.
   He probably won't say anything.

d He's going to fall.
   What's going to happen?

⌹ Now listen and check your answers.

22 Around the world

1 Where in the world?

A
B
C
D
E

1 You will hear five people talking about the places in the pictures.

a Look at the pictures. Whereabouts in the world do you think each place is?

b Look at the words in the box. Which words do you think each speaker will use?

c 📼 Now listen to the tape. Where does each speaker come from? What does he or she say about each place?

mountains	island	farmland
coast	forest	volcano
valley	canal	border
desert	beach	lake

2 Choose one of the following:
– the place you come from
– a place you'd like to live

Say where it is and what it's like.

2 Visiting time

1 You're thinking of visiting Egypt. When do you think is the best time of the year to go?
   – March? – August? – November?
   Read the text and find out.

Egypt

The climate of Egypt is mainly hot and dry. Apart from the Valley of the River Nile, which runs through the country from south to north, it consists entirely of desert.

In the summer, the temperature often reaches 45° in the south of the country, and 30° in the north.

In winter, the weather is cooler, and along the north coast it is often cloudy, with occasional rain.

In Cairo it rains on average for three days a year, and in the south of Egypt rain is almost unknown. There are often gentle breezes from the north throughout the year, except during March and April, when a hot, dusty wind blows from the south.

Make a list of words from the text that are related to *climate*. Add some more words of your own.

2 When is the best time of the year to visit your country? Why?

3 Countries, nationalities and languages

1 Complete the first part of the table. Add the names of three more countries. Ask another student to fill in the nationalities and the languages.

2 Work in pairs. Choose a country and write one sentence about it on a piece of paper. Pass it to another pair. They will add a sentence and pass it on.

Morocco

It borders on the Sahara desert.
It's a very hot country.
The people speak Arabic.
It's in North Africa.
The capital city is Rabat.
It's famous for its leather.
Couscous is one of the national dishes.

They're from …	They're …	They speak …
Italy	Italian	Italian
Japan		Japanese
	Danish	Danish
Iraq	Iraqi	
Brazil		
	Canadian	
Mexico		
	Austrian	
Vietnam		
1		
2		
3		

4 Car chaos

READING

1 **Read the text about Lagos and answer these questions:**

    a Why is there a traffic problem in Lagos?

    b What did the Government do about it?

    c What's special about Wednesdays?

2 **Read the text again, and decide if these sentences are true or false.**

    a Until the mid-1970s only rich people in Lagos had cars.

    b The best days to do business in Lagos are Tuesday and Thursday.

    c The new law was a complete failure from the start.

    d Some car owners drive into Lagos every day.

    e Traffic was worse in the mid-1970s than it is now.

LISTENING

 You will hear about some solutions to traffic problems around the world. Listen and make notes about these countries:

– Italy
– Singapore
– The Netherlands
– Britain
– The United States
– Hong Kong

Think about traffic in your own country. What are the problems? What are the solutions?

Wednesday is an odd day in Lagos

Most capital cities have fallen victim to the car. O'seun Ogunseitan reports from Nigeria where traffic in Lagos has come to a virtual standstill.

Try not to schedule business appointments in Lagos on a Wednesday – particularly if you have to cross one of the many bridges into the commercial centre, 'the Island'. It is not that Wednesdays are work-free days in Lagos. Just the opposite: mid-week is now the day Lagos roads are busiest.

In 1977, when the city's population was about four million, no fewer than two million people hit Lagos roads at the same time, generally going to the same place – the Island. Two million people filled the city's roads in every conceivable kind of vehicle: buses, mini-buses, taxis, mini-taxis and of course, cars, cars and more cars.

Car ownership shot up in the oil boom of the mid-1970s. Before anybody realised what was happening, nearly all middle-income workers in business and in the civil service, even teachers and clerks, had joined the rich in the car owners' club. Every day more than 150,000 cars contributed to the traffic headache.

The State Government decided to take action. It enacted an ingenious traffic control law which divided the cars on Lagos streets into two groups – based on whether they had registration numbers starting with odd or even numbers. On Mondays, Wednesdays and Fridays, only the odd-numbered cars can use the roads. On Tuesdays and Thursdays cars with registration numbers beginning with 2, 4, 6 or 8 are permitted.

The first problem is that there will always be more cars on the road on the 'odd-number' days, because there are more odd than even digits – no registration numbers in Nigeria start with zero.

But on Mondays, things are not too bad. The week is still young and business activities are still fairly quiet. Then on Friday, Jumat prayers by Moslems mean that the day virtually ends at noon. So Friday is quiet as well. Wednesday is therefore the choice day when as many people as possible – and as many odd-numbered vehicles as possible – are on the move. Traffic is a nightmare.

This law had many interesting effects. Some former car owners, for example, became hitch-hikers. And neighbours with odd- and even-numbered cars suddenly became more friendly, giving each other rides to work on the alternate days when their cars had no right to the road.

But soon the richer Lagosians found another solution. They began to buy second cars so they had a car each for the odd and even number days and could therefore drive into the city when they liked.

By 1980, second cars had become so common that the traffic control law became virtually useless. Since then the traffic chaos has gone from bad to worse. Today 200,000 cars compete daily for the 50,000 available parking spaces on the Island. The population of Lagos – a tiny stretch of coastal land 35 kilometres wide and ten kilometres long – has ballooned to eight million.

Lagos struggles on in the stranglehold of the motor car.

O'seun Ogunseitan is a Nigerian journalist.

1 Up to now

Present perfect continuous & simple • for & since

1 Look at these conversations.
   Complete the replies, using the verb in brackets.

   What is the difference between *for* and *since*?

Hello. You live next door, don't you?

Yes. We (*live*) there since January.

Have you only just arrived?

No. I (*be*) here since 2 o'clock.

Do you know them well?

Oh yes. We (*know*) them for about 5 years.

I hear you play golf.

Yes. I (*play*) for about 6 months now.

2 Now complete these conversations.

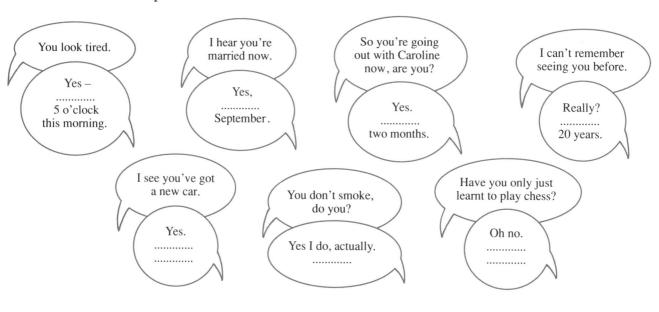

You look tired.

Yes –
....
5 o'clock
this morning.

I hear you're married now.

Yes,
....
September.

So you're going out with Caroline now, are you?

Yes.
....
two months.

I can't remember seeing you before.

Really?
....
20 years.

I see you've got a new car.

Yes.
....
....

You don't smoke, do you?

Yes I do, actually.
....

Have you only just learnt to play chess?

Oh no.
....
....

2 How long?

Questions

We've got a dog.
I study Russian at university.
I collect stamps.

I'm married.
My sister works in New York.
I play the guitar.

I go to evening classes.
I'm in the local football team.
My brother's in the army.

1 What questions might you ask these people with *How long...?*

2 Write three sentences about yourself, and pass them to another student.
Ask and answer questions. Include some questions with *How long...?*

3 A slice of life

spend (+ -ing) • for • from ... to / till

How much of your day do you spend sleeping? working? eating? talking to people? What else do you do? **We** asked Andy Powell, a 22-year-old economics student at London University, how he divides up his day.

Work: I go to lectures from 9 till 12, and I have classes from 2 to 4. Apart from that I spend about 3 hours in the library or working in my room.

Travel: My flat's near the university. I don't spend more than half an hour a day travelling.

Eating: I don't eat breakfast, and I only have time for a quick lunch. Dinner's more relaxed. I suppose I spend about 2 hours altogether having meals.

Friends: I go out nearly every night for 4 hours or so. We usually meet in a pub and go on somewhere.

Reading: I don't read much apart from work. I read a bit in bed – maybe half an hour a day.

TV: I watch TV for about an hour a day on average. I usually watch the news, and sometimes there's a good movie or music programme.

Sleep: I go to bed pretty late usually. I probably sleep about 6 hours a night – from 2 till 8.

That makes 22 hours out of 24. So how does Andy spend the other 2?
Doing nothing!

1 Complete the pie-chart with information from the text.

2 How did you divide up your day yesterday?
Complete the pie-chart on page 123.
Then compare your chart with your partner's.

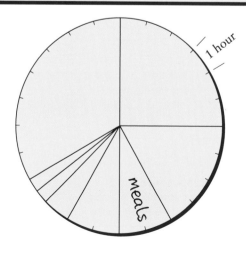

4 Murder in the office

10.00: Mrs Green calls to see her husband at his office.

10.45: Mr Green phones the police: his wife is lying dead, with a knife in her back.

11.00: The police arrive. There are four people in the office …

1 Listen to the tape and make notes in the table.

2 Who do you think murdered Mrs Green?

The suspects	9.00	9.30	10.00	10.30	11.00	Notes
Mr Green the manager						
Mrs White the accountant						
Miss Brown the secretary						
Mr Black the sales rep						

Grammar Checklist

Present perfect continuous tense

have/has + been + -ing

He's **been** living here since 1990.
   (*not* ~~He's living here since 1990.~~)
I've **been** waiting for hours.
   (*not* ~~I'm waiting~~ …)

for & since

for + *periods of time*; **since** + *points of time*

He's been here **for** an hour / **for** 3 days / **for** years. (*not* ~~since an hour.~~)
He's been here **since** 2.30 / **since** May / **since** 1950.

Questions

have/has + *subject* + **been** + **-ing**

Have you **been** waiting long?
How long **have** you **been** waiting?
   (*not* ~~How long you have been~~ …)

Stative verbs

No continuous form – use Present perfect simple
be, have (*= possess*)**, know**

I've **known** her for years.
   (*not* … ~~been knowing~~ …)
They've **been** here since September.
How long have you **had** your car?

spend (+ -ing)

She **spent** two years in India.
They **spend** most evenings play**ing** cards.

Duration prepositions

He worked **from** 9 | **till** 12.
                 | **to** 12.
He worked **for** 3 hours.

See also Reference section, page 141.

Focus on Form

1 Simple or continuous?

I've		for 2 hours.
She's	....	
They've		for a year.

Make sentences from the table using the phrases below.

Examples:

talk on the phone
They've been talking on the phone for 2 hours.

have a headache
I've had a headache for 2 hours.

a know him
b read the paper
c live here
d have a car
e have dinner
f play chess
g be a taxi driver
h learn Portuguese

2 For & since

Add *for* or *since* to the phrases in the box.

.... a few minutes	.... a week
.... three hours	.... last June
.... 6 o'clock	.... Christmas
.... yesterday morning	.... three years
.... Friday	.... a long time
.... several days	 1948

Use three of the phrases in sentences of your own.

3 Questions: How long ...?

How long have you	past participle	... ?
	been + -ing	

1 Look at the pictures. What can you tell about the people?

2 Ask and answer questions with *How long ...?*

A How long have you been playing the violin?
B For about 10 years.

A How long have you had your violin?
B Since Christmas.

4 Spending time

Change these sentences (if necessary) so that they are true of you.

a I spend most of my time out of doors.
b I spend about two hours a day in the bathroom.
c I'm going to spend next weekend working.
d I spent last Sunday watching TV in bed.
e I don't spend much time keeping fit.

5 Pronunciation

How do you say the words and phrases below?

a for an hour   for 3 months   for about 5 years
We've known them for about 5 years.

b since September   since 2 o'clock   since 1948
He's been waiting since 2 o'clock.

c How long has she known him?
How long have you been living here?

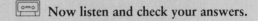 Now listen and check your answers.

---

24 But is it art?

1 Art forms

Which pairs go together? Match the numbers and the letters. What's the connection between them?

B

C

D

161 HENRY MOORE *Reclining Mother and Child* 1960–1

E

F

Mills & Boon
ROMANCE
One Secret Too Many
VANESSA GRANT

G

THE·PENGUIN·BOOK·OF
AMERICAN
VERSE
EDITED·BY·GEOFFREY·MOORE

SUNOCO

REVISED·EDITION

H

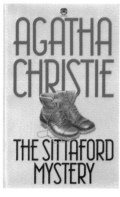

AGATHA CHRISTIE
THE SITTAFORD MYSTERY

I

9.40 **Gone with the Wind.** Clark Gable and Vivien Leigh star in this 1939 blockbuster set in the American Civil War.

J

2 Who's who?

1 The teacher will read a description of a well known person. You will hear five sentences altogether. After each sentence, write down who you think the person is.

Guess 1	
Guess 2	
Guess 3	
Guess 4	
Guess 5	

2 Work with a partner. Together, think of a well known person, and write five sentences about him/her. Your person can be

a novelist	a composer	a sculptor
a singer	a poet	a musician
an actor	a playwright	a painter

Read your sentences one at a time to another pair, and see if they can guess who it is.

1

WHERE DID YOU GET TO?
WHAT WAS HER NAME?
DID SHE KNOW SHE WAS PLAYING
ONE OF YOUR GAMES?
DO YOU THINK OF THE HEARTACHE
DO YOU THINK OF THE HURT
WHEN I WANT YOU TO LOVE ME
AND YOU TREAT ME LIKE DIRT?
AND ONE OF THESE DAYS
I'M GOIN' TO BREAK DOWN THE DOOR,
ENOUGH IS ENOUGH
AND I CAN'T TAKE ANY MORE,
AND ONE OF THESE DAYS
I'M GOIN' TO SAY GOODBYE –
THERE'S LOTS OF LIVIN' TO DO
BEFORE I DIE …

2

'Have you any idea,' he said, breathing hard, 'how long he's been dead?'

'About two hours, I should say, or possibly three.'

Burnaby passed his tongue over dry lips.

'Would you say,' he asked, 'that he might have been killed at five twenty-five?'

The doctor looked at him curiously.

3

This Is Just to Say

I have eaten
the plums
that were in
the icebox

and which
you were probably
saving
for breakfast

Forgive me
they were delicious
so sweet
and so cold.

4 ❦ Carmen: Act 1 ❦

Carmen is a story of love and betrayal. Don José, an army brigadier, is engaged to Micaela, a village girl. Act 1 is set in a street in Seville, and begins with a lively chorus of soldiers. Micaela appears

5

6

7

8

needed her. He said, slowly and with difficulty, 'Alex, I've never been in love before.'

She was very still. His eyes closed, then opened again, meeting hers. She swallowed and said, 'Sam, you don't have to say it.'

'I love you,' he said, very softly, 'I've loved you for

9

Copyright © 1990 DC Comics Inc.

10

hammering and coughing. MASHA *and* MEDVIEDENKO, *returning from a walk, enter from the left.*]

MEDVIEDENKO. Why do you always wear black?

MASHA. I'm in mourning for my life. I'm unhappy.

MEDVIEDENKO. But why? [*Meditatively.*] I can't understand it. You're in good health. Your father isn't rich, but

3 Pictures at an exhibition

Look at the pictures on the next two pages.

1 Which of these words would you use to describe each picture?

attractive	ugly	interesting
beautiful	silly	meaningless

2 Imagine someone gave you reproductions of all the pictures.
  Which would you put on your wall? Which wall?

3 Choose the picture you like the best. Why do you like it?
  What's the most striking thing about it? What does it make you think of?

Street Scene 1935 L.S. Lowry

Woman's Head with Sombrero 1962 Pablo Picasso

Painting 1937 Ben Nicholson

Landschaft am Meer 1914 August Macke

Circus Girl Georges Rouault (1871–1958)

Icarus 1947 Henri Matisse

4 The Night in the Hotel

READING

Read the story in your own time. Focus on these questions:
- What does the porter tell Schwamm?
- What happens when Schwamm enters his room?
- Why has Schwamm come to the city?
- What does the stranger tell Schwamm?
- What does Schwamm do the next day?
- What does the stranger do the next day?

THE NIGHT IN THE HOTEL

by Siegfried Lenz

The night porter shrugged his shoulders.

'That's all there is,' he said. 'One free bed in a double room. At this time of night you won't find a single room anywhere.'

5 'Very well,' said Schwamm. 'I'll take the bed, only ... well, I'd like to know with whom I have to share the room. Is my ... partner – is he already there?'

'Yes he is and he's already asleep.'

'Asleep,' Schwamm repeated.

10 Taking the registration form he filled it in and handed it back to the porter. Then he went upstairs. Schwamm slowed his step as he saw the door with the correct room number, held his breath in the hope that he could hear the stranger, and bent down over the
15 keyhole. The room was dark.

Schwamm pressed the door handle down, closed the door behind him and felt for the light-switch with a flat hand. There he stopped. Nearby someone spoke:

'Stop! Please leave the light off. You would do me a great favour if you left the room dark.' 20

'Were you waiting for me?' asked Schwamm, shaken. But he received no reply. Instead the stranger carried on:

'Don't trip over my crutches, and watch you don't fall over my suitcase; it's lying roughly in the middle 25 of the room. I'll direct you safely to your bed: take three steps along the wall, then turn left, and when you've taken another three steps you'll be able to touch the bedpost.'

Schwamm obeyed. He reached the bed, took off his 30 clothes and slid under the covers. He heard the soft breaths of the stranger and knew that he would never be able to get to sleep.

'By the way,' he said hesitantly, after a while. 'My name is Schwamm.' 35

'Uh-huh,' said the stranger.

'Yes.'

'Did you come here for a conference?'

'No, and you?'

'No.' 40

'On business?' asked Schwamm.

'Not really.'

'I've probably got the most remarkable reason a man could have for travelling to this city,' said Schwamm. 45

In the railway station a train started to move. The ground trembled and the beds on which the two men lay vibrated.

'Do you want to commit suicide in the city?' asked the stranger. 50

'No!' Schwamm replied. 'Do I look like it?'

'I don't know how you look,' said the other man. 'It's dark in here.'

'God forbid, no,' Schwamm explained. 'I have a son, mister...er... (the stranger didn't give his name) 55 ... a little rascal, and I came here because of him.'

'Is he in hospital?'

'Heavens no, why do you say that? He's quite healthy. But he's exceptionally sensitive you see. He even reacts when a shadow falls on him.' 60

'Ah, so he is in a hospital.'

'No!' cried Schwamm. 'I've already told you that he's healthy in every respect, but he's in danger. The little rascal has a soul of glass – that's the problem.'

'So why doesn't he commit suicide?' asked the 65 stranger.

'What do you mean? A child like that, at his age; how can you say such a thing? No. I'll tell you why my son is in danger. Each morning as he goes to
70 school – he always goes alone, by the way – each morning he has to stand by a level crossing and wait until the early train has passed. The little fellow just stands there and waves and waves like mad, so happy and yet despondent.'
75 'So?'
'Then,' Schwamm continued, 'he goes to school, and when he comes back he's disturbed and confused, and sometimes even weeping. He can't do his schoolwork, he doesn't want to play or even speak.
80 This has been going on for months now, every blasted day!'
'What got him into this state?'
'Well,' said Schwamm, 'it's peculiar really: the boy waves and – you should see his sad little face – and
85 none of the passengers wave back at him. And he takes it to heart so much that we – my wife and I – are afraid something might happen. He waves, and no-one waves back.'

'So you, mister Schwamm, want to help your son by
90 taking the early train so you can wave at him?'
'Yes,' said Schwamm. 'Yes.'
'For myself,' said the stranger, 'I can't bear children. I hate them and avoid them at all costs. I lost my wife because of children. She died in childbirth – our first.'

'I'm sorry,' said Schwamm. A cosy warmth flooded   95
his body; he felt that at last he would be able to sleep.

The stranger asked: 'You're going to Kurzbach, right?'
'Yes.'
'And you're not at all worried about what you're
about to do? Aren't you ashamed of cheating your   100
son?'
Schwamm retorted:
'Where on earth did you get that idea from?' He
sank back into the bed and pulled the covers over his
head, lay for a while thinking, and fell asleep.   105

When he woke the next morning Schwamm realised
that he was alone in the room. He glanced at his
watch and started. The early train was due to go in
five minutes. There was no way he could catch it.

That afternoon – he couldn't bear to spend another   110
day in the city – he arrived back home depressed and
disappointed. His son opened the door and threw
himself against Schwamm and hammered on his thighs
with his fists.
'Someone waved! Someone waved for ages and   115
ages!'
'Who?' asked Schwamm ... 'A man with a crutch?'
'Yes, yes. He waved his stick, then he tied a hankie
to it and held it out the window until I couldn't see it
any more!'   120

LISTENING

📼 **Listen to the story and follow the text.**

Is there anything that is strange or unexpected in the story?

Do you think this is a good story? Why (or why not)?

Revision and extension

1

At an international conference, someone asks you the best time of year to visit your country. What do you say?

2

A friend of yours is taking his/her driving test next week. Tell him or her what to expect. (If you don't know, ask questions instead.)

3

At a party you're introduced to a newly married couple who are both teachers and who have recently moved to your town. Think of three questions you might ask them.

4

Talk about one of these topics. Can you keep talking for one minute?

trains

myself

jokes

seasons

10 years from now

the world

dreams

old films

murder

good books

5 Once upon a time ...

Work in a group. Make up a story together. Try to include as many of these ideas as you can.

6 True or false?

1 On a piece of paper, write ten sentences about yourself. Five should be true and five should be false. Choose topics in the box.

2 Give the piece of paper to the person sitting next to you. Can he/she tell which sentences are true and which are false?

where you come from	what languages you speak
your job	your favourite kind of music
your age	countries you've visited
your family	what you're going to do this weekend
your leisure activities	a book you're reading at the moment
your personality	what you did yesterday evening
a problem you have	something important that's happened to you recently

Additional material

9·1 Find the difference *Student A*

11·4 Round trip *Map C*

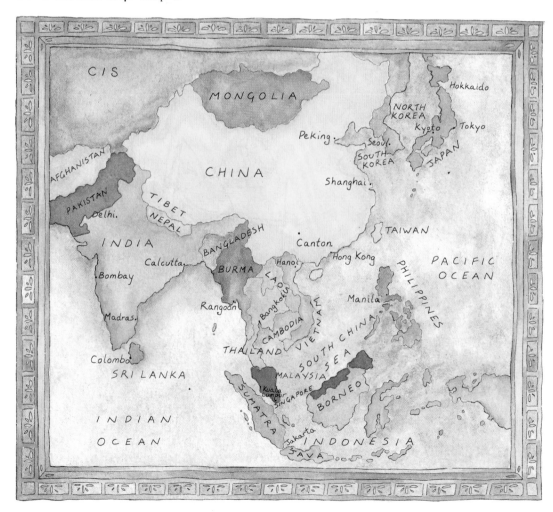

1·Focus on Form·1 *Picture A*

5·4 Cartoons *Group A*

traffic jam
umbrella

'Do you mind if I shelter from the rain? I am waiting for a friend.'

7·3 Aesop's fables *Student A*

The Wind and the Sun

One day, the Wind and the Sun had an argument.

'I'm stronger than you,' said the Wind, and blew as hard as he could.

'Nonsense,' said the Sun.

Just then they saw a man walking along wearing a hat and a coat.

'I'll show you how strong I am,' said the Wind. 'Watch me blow that man's hat and coat off.' He blew and blew, but the man only pulled his hat over his ears and held onto his coat.

'Now it's my turn,' said the Sun, and he came out from behind a cloud and shone down on the man.

'Whew, it's getting hot!' said the man. He took his hat and coat off, and lay down on the ground and fell asleep.

'I've won,' said the Sun, quietly.

Moral: Force isn't always necessary.

9·1 Find the differences *Student B*

11·4 Round trip *Map A*

1·Focus on Form·1 *Picture B*

5·4 Cartoons *Group B*

forest
bear
sleeping bag

"Sandwiches!"

7·3 Aesop's fables *Student B*

The Horse and the Donkey

One day, a man went on a journey, and took with him his horse and his donkey. He put a very heavy load on the donkey's back, but nothing on the horse's back. After a while, the poor donkey asked the horse to help him. But the horse, who was very selfish, refused.

Further along the road, the donkey started to feel very tired, and again asked the horse to take some of the load. And again the horse refused.

Finally, the donkey fell exhausted at the side of the road and died. So the man took the whole of the heavy load and put it on the horse's back, together with the skin of the dead donkey, and they continued on their journey.

Moral: You get nothing from being selfish.

5·4 Cartoons *Group C*

sink
desert island
portable phone

11·4 Round trip *Map B*

Additional material

13·2 General knowledge *Student A*

Ask *Which...?* questions based on these facts:

1 The temperature in Rio de Janeiro in summer is about 29°C; in winter it's about 17°C.
   The temperature in Hong Kong in summer is about 28°C; in winter in it's about 15°C.

2 A human being has 32 teeth.
   A crocodile has 64 teeth.

3 Mont Blanc is 4807 metres high.
   Mount Kilimanjaro is 5894 metres haigh.

4 The Kremlin was built in 1156.
   Buckingham Palace was built in 1705.

14·2 Can you tell me the way to...? *Student A*

You're at the railway station.

Ask B the way to

– the bank
– the swimming pool
– the Regal Hotel

When you find out where they are, mark them on the map.

13·2 General knowledge *Student B*

Ask *Which...?* questions based on these facts:

1 The United States of America measures nearly $9\frac{1}{2}$ million square kilometres.
   Canada measures nearly 10 million square kilometres.

2 The Greek alphabet has 24 letters.
   The Russian alphabet has 33 letters.

3 The Suez Canal is 162 kilometres long.
   The Panama Canal is 82 kilometres long.

4 The Atlantic Ocean is 3,300 metres deep, on average.
   The Pacific Ocean is 4,000 metres deep, on average.

14·2 Can you tell me the way to...? *Student B*

You're at the railway station.

Ask A the way to:

– the Ritz Hotel
– the library
– the tennis courts

When you find out where they are, mark them on the map.

19·3 Mystery flight *Student A*

Washington lawyer in flight mystery

Thomas Root, a lawyer and experienced pilot, left Washington early on Thursday morning in his Cessna light aircraft. He was on a routine business trip to visit a client in Rocky Mount, a town 156 miles away.

Just before he reached Rocky Mount, he radioed to say that he was suffering from pains in the chest. And that was the last air traffic controllers heard from the plane.

As the plane continued to fly south on autopilot at 10,000 feet, the US Air Force sent two planes to intercept it, and they saw Mr Root lying unconscious at the controls. The officers in charge assumed that Mr Root had had a heart attack. Hoping that he might still be alive, they sent a plane carrying parachutists to rescue Mr Root when the Cessna eventually crashed into the sea.

(Adapted from *The Times*, Saturday 15 July 1989)

20·2 How old? *Student A*

Washington lawyer in flight mystery

Six hours after taking off, the airplane finally ran out of fuel over the Bahamas and crashed into the sea 14 miles from Eleuthera Island. Miraculously, Mr Root survived. "He just popped right up in the water. He swam to us. He could talk", said Captain Raymond Walizer, co-pilot of a helicopter at the scene.

Mr Root was immediately taken to hospital. Doctors found that his lungs were full of carbon monoxide – but they also found a gunshot wound in his left side. Police believe that Mr Root was shot at close range while he was in the air.

Mrs Kathy Root followed her husband's ghostly journey with their three chldren aged 7, 4 and 18 months. She had this message for her husband when doctors told her he was still alive: "Root, you really did it this time".

(Adapted from *The Times*, Saturday 15 July 1989)

20·2 How old? *Student B*

17·4 Personal problems

My son steals

My guess is that your son is crying out for more attention and love from you. Until he was 7, he was the only child, and had you all to himself. Now, you say, you all do things together – that is, he has to share you with his little sister. Does he ever get to spend time alone with you, without her? If not, he may feel that you don't love him as much as you once did. Try to put aside some time every day especially for him – perhaps after his sister's bedtime – and ask your husband to do the same. If your son feels that he's an important part of your lives, he may stop stealing – and he'll like his little sister more, too.

She doesn't like me

You don't say how long this has been going on. Your new manager may feel that it's best to be very hard at the beginning, to 'show who's boss', and after a week or two she may begin to feel more confident and relax a little.

If you think that's not the answer, you should make an appointment to speak to her privately. Ask her what she thinks about your work, and find out exactly what she likes and doesn't like. The problem may be something that you can sort out easily. If not – well, maybe you should look for another job.

Will she pay?

It's possible that your girlfriend has a good reason for not paying you back yet, but doesn't want to tell you. Perhaps she isn't earning as much as you think. Perhaps she's helping out her parents with money. Perhaps she thinks you'll leave her once you've got your money back. On the other hand, it's possible that she has no good reason at all.

Whatever the situation, it's important that you sit down and discuss the problem as soon as possible, before it has a serious effect on your relationship. Of course, you could end up losing both your girlfriend and your money, but if you do nothing that's probably going to happen anyway.

23·3 A slice of life

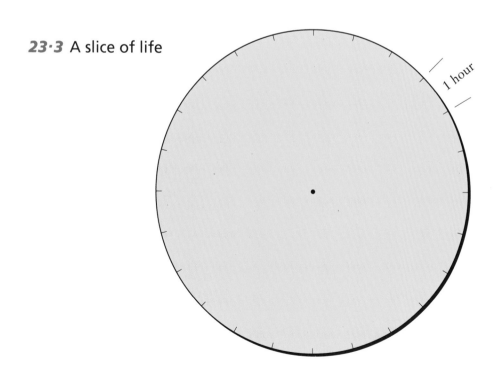

1 hour

Tapescripts

1·3 Hotel

Yes, well I love this hotel, in fact I always go there. There's a very good restaurant, there's a bar where you can sit and talk to people, relax. The rooms have got telephones and there's a fax service, just what you need on a business trip. And it's near the airport so it's very convenient.

Well it's not bad, but er it's not all that great. The rooms are comfortable, but I think they're very expensive. It's a long way from the centre of town, um but there's a nice garden to sit in, um but no tennis courts, no swimming pool. The restaurant's good, but um again I think it's quite expensive.

Well, I really like staying there. The rooms are very comfortable; and you have a big bathroom, which I like; and a television in your room and the beds are very comfortable, which is important. You can also get breakfast in bed, er or at least in your room in the morning. And I always have a room at the back, which is nice and quiet. And they've got lovely gardens at the back too.

2·1 Photo album

Oh, this is a lovely one. This is Julie and David and me. That's David in the middle – he's my boyfriend, and he's a writer. And then that's me, on the right hand side, and Julie er on the left hand side – she's a secretary, we met at work.

Oh, this one's very nice, too. This is my grandmother. I think it was taken at a wedding. Do you know she's nearly 80? She doesn't look it, does she?

Oh and then this one, this is another one of my boyfriend, David – he's just behind me, do you see? And that's my older brother, in the black jacket – he's 23 now, and he's an actor. And then next to him is his girlfriend – isn't she lovely? She's an actress.

Oh and this one is my baby brother! His name's Jack. I don't see a lot of him, which is a pity, because he's with Mum and Dad in Scotland.

2·4 Are you a loner?

1 I live in a, in a town, um actually it's rather a quiet suburb as it happens, but it's also not too far from, from the centre, so I can, I can get into the centre in about 10 minutes, I suppose.
2 When I was younger I used to have um a party quite often. Nowadays I like just to go out for a meal, really, um with my wife or perhaps a couple of friends, just to go out for a meal.
3 I like to be somewhere warm um and beautiful, and not too crowded. Um so that usually means flying somewhere with my family, um but of course it's getting more and more difficult to find somewhere beautiful and warm and quiet.
4 I think probably I would talk to my friend quite a lot, at least at the beginning of the evening, maybe later I would um I hope meet a couple of people.
5 Yes, well once I did spend New Year's Eve alone. I was living abroad, and I had nothing to do, and I went to an English pub, and it was very noisy and I didn't know anybody, and I left very quickly, it wasn't very nice. And I caught a bus home, and the New Year happened on the bus, and the other people on the bus all smiled and said Happy New Year, and it was a very happy occasion, although all of us were in fact alone.
6 I think when I was bit younger, I think no. Um but now, now that I'm married and I have a family um I think I would enjoy these a lot more because I am not alone very much. Um swimming, no, I don't think – maybe I wouldn't cook a big meal just for myself. Um but the others, yes – especially a weekend alone at home would be lovely.

3·1 Lifestyles

A So this is a lovely café. Is it a family business?
B Yeah, you see, my parents cook the food and I help there serving the customers. I've got an older brother too but he comes only when it's very busy, for example at the weekends.
A And do you work here all year round?
B No, no, it's only open during the summer. In winter my parents have got a farm and we work there. Um I also study economics at university.
A And does your brother work on the farm too?
B No, he works on a ship during the winter, because there you can earn a lot of money.

3·3 When do you wear ... ?

I usually wear a tie to work. Um I don't wear one at home normally, except if we have very important visitors or something. Er but I nearly always wear a tie when I go out for a meal or to the theatre or to the cinema or something like that.

I don't usually wear a tie, but um if I'm going out to a party or a meal or a wedding, formal occasion like that then, yes, I will wear a tie, but but not usually.

Well unfortunately er I have to wear a tie to the office, but er I hate the things and I generally tend to put it on before I go into the office and take it off immediately I come out. I certainly don't wear them at home, unless it's a special occasion.

4·2 On the move

1 A Where do you want to go?
  B The airport, please.
  A Okay.
2 A Return to Manchester, please.
  B That's £34, please.
  A Thank you. Oh – where do I go?
  B Platform 3 – it leaves in five minutes.
3 A Just one suitcase, is it?
  B Yes.
  A Okay. And do you want smoking or non-smoking?
  B Non-smoking, please.
4 A Yes, sir.
  B Forty litres of super, please.
  A Forty, right.
5 A Do you go to the town centre?
  B Yes. 60 pence, please.
  A Thanks.
6 Your attention please, ladies and gentlemen. We are now approaching Madrid. Will all passengers please return to their seats and fasten their seat belts. Thank you.

4·4 Airport

Although I enjoy um airports, I usually feel slightly nervous and worried because there is a flight. In airports um I find it's it's necessary always to to stay near the the departures or the arrivals notice boards so that you're always quite um sure that when you have to go to your gate that you're going to go at the right time and not get lost.

I normally feel very bored when I'm waiting at airports. Flights always seem to be delayed these days, anyway, so you have to wait for very long periods. Um if I've remembered to take a good book with me, I sometimes sit there and read, um or else I suppose I would maybe go and wander round some of the shops or wander round looking at the duty free goods for sale.

I always find airports very exciting places to be. I like the whole atmosphere, I like the feeling of people travelling, going to far-away places, it's just really exciting. I really enjoy waiting at airports, I like to wander round, see the planes taking off and landing, looking around seeing where people are going, what people are doing, I find it very easy to fill up the time at airports usually.

Well I fly a lot between here and Australia so waiting at airports is just a normal thing for me. Luckily I love to read, I always take a good book with me, and er if I'm held up, if a flight's delayed, which often happens with me, then it's a chance to have a good read.

5·3 The whole picture

Well, this is a picture of a beach. There are a lot of people sitting, talking, drinking. Maybe in the sea there are some children swimming and playing in the water and perhaps further up the beach there's a kiosk with people selling things.

I think in this picture there are probably more boats, there are probably boats on the beach and boats in the water. There are people lying on the beach sunbathing, er there's a group of teenagers playing football, erm there's a policeman keeping an eye on everybody.

Maybe behind the beach there's a street and there are people walking along the street looking in the shops, shops selling various things, perhaps souvenirs or ice-creams. And there are cars driving along and the drivers looking at the people on the beach maybe.

6·3 Eating out

A (and B) Good evening.
C Good evening. Have you reserved a table?
A No, I'm afraid we haven't.
C Um what about this table by the window?
A Yes, that'll be fine, thanks.
C Are you ready to order now?
B Yes, I think so. I'll have the chicken, please.
A And I'll have the fish.
C What would you like to drink?
A Just mineral water, please.
B Mm. That was a lovely meal.
A Yes it was, wasn't it? Er, could we have the bill, please?

6·4 Cholesterol and your heart

A Do you think you're basically a, a pretty healthy person?
B Yes, I get a cold once every three years and you know that's about it.
A And do you think that's because of er what you eat and er the exercise you take?

B Um I don't know. I mean I, I like food and I eat, I think I eat healthy food, I don't like sweets very much and I eat raw food and I eat fruit and vegetables and lots of salad, but too much, too much of everything.
A What about smoking? Do you smoke?
B No, I've never smoked at all.
A Do you drink alcohol?
B Yes, but only wine and you know with meals.
A And do you take regular exercise?
B Um not enough. In summer I ride a bicycle, and in winter I try to do some swimming regularly, but um I really ought to be more disciplined about it.
A Steve, you look extremely healthy. Do you think you are a healthy person?
B Um well I feel healthy, um I have a healthy outlook on life, I'm not too bad.
A And what about smoking. Do you smoke?
B Yes, I do. Um not a great deal, um but usually in the evenings if I'm with friends, in the pub for example, I would say I smoke between 10 and 15 a day, which isn't too bad.
A Right and and what about your diet? Do you think it's healthy? Do you watch your fat and cholesterol levels all the time?
B Not really, no because um I sort of enjoy the taste of things too much, the things that I'm not supposed to eat, like red meat and fried food and, you know dairy products, which I enjoy, so it's not the world's healthiest diet, no.
A Right. And what about exercise? Do you jog or play tennis or anything?
B Um I play football once a week, if I can, and when I can avoid getting a bus, you know I try and walk places. So that's about the only exercise I do.

7·2 Getting the details

A Hello. When did you get back?
B Um this morning. About three o'clock.
A Did you have a good time?
B It was brilliant, yeah. Really good.
C How did you go, by train?
B No, I needed the car, so I drove there, yeah.
C Hm. And did you stop at all on the way?
B Yeah, just once, for something to eat, and that's all.
D Did you go to Vienna?
B Yes, I was in Vienna the whole time, so um (laughs) I saw a lot of Vienna.
D Where did you stay?
B With friends that had invited me to er, to go and visit them. And they showed me round Vienna, um so they were my holiday guides.

8·3 Personal space

I like this room. I like the fact that it's very simple, that the whole room is one colour, that there's very little clutter, very little furniture, very few ornaments. But I would add some plants and flowers to give it a little more life, I think.

It's a bit bare for my liking, a bit too much like a prison cell. Um I quite like things to be simple, but this is slightly depressing. Um I'd certainly change the picture on the wall, and I think it could do with a rug or two, and if possible a sidelight, like a lamp-stand rather than the overhead light.

The room's got very good light. Um I like the size of the window. But the furniture's all hard and uncomfortable, and the colours are gloomy. So I think I'd have to paint it white or something, or at least pale. And that horrible fire – ugh, it makes me feel cold just to look at it.

8·4 Haunted houses

This happened when I was about three years old. I can't have been any more than that because I don't actually remember it myself, but my parents told me about it afterwards. Well, we had a cellar underneath the house where my mother did the washing, and I said I wanted to look in this little room at the side, you see we had a little room where we kept coal. And so we went inside, and it was empty and dark, and I said, 'Oh look at that lady in the corner.' And I described an old lady in the corner. She had grey hair and she was wearing a coloured apron, but I was the only person who could see this woman. And so we went back upstairs very quickly, and my mother wouldn't go down in the cellar again for three weeks after that. And then later, my parents were talking to the neighbours about it, and they said, 'Well, did you know that the woman who lived in the house before you was this rather strange old lady, and she had grey hair and she always wore a coloured apron. And she died in the cellar.'

9·1 Find the differences

A Well on the plate there are some bananas and an orange.
B What about grapes?
A No, there aren't any grapes.
B What's on the table?
A On the table – there are some plates, and some bread and a bottle of – wine, I think.
B Can you see any cheese in your picture?
A Yes. There's some cheese on the shelf.
B Are there any glasses?
A Glasses? Yes. Three glasses.

B Any cups?
A No, I can't see any cups.

9·3 What's the problem?

We're building 500,000 new houses in the cities because at the moment there aren't enough houses available for a reasonable rent. There are far too many people sleeping on the streets, especially young people, and we feel it's very important to create more homes which will be available for a reasonable rent.

Well of course I know a lot of people are very upset about this school closing down, but there are simply too many schools in the area, and not enough children to fill them. So what we're doing is we're closing down the smallest of the schools and bussing the children to the next town.

There are so many take-away shops and things of that nature now that people's eating habits are changing and not for the better, I'm afraid. People are eating too much fat, too much sugar, and not enough fresh fruit and vegetables. If you want a quick snack between meals you'd be much much better to eat a piece of fruit.

10·2 Clothes quiz

A Ooh Anne, I like that denim jacket there. What, what do you think of it?
B Ooh yes, it's nice. I love the colour. How much is it?
A Um, £40.
B That's not too bad. Go on, [gap].
A Right. There. Well, what do you think?
B Ooh I think it [gap], it's great. And it really [gap] your trousers. What does it feel like?
A Oh it's very comfortable. Um it's right, the right length, seems to [gap] very well. Yeah, I think I'll [gap].

10·4 Going for gold

A I see you're wearing a pendant. Where does it come from?
B Well I bought this when I was living in Egypt. I was living in Cairo for a few years, and I was wandering around the souk there one afternoon, which is the market. And it's a huge market, and one part of it is a gold market. And I was looking in one of the shop windows and I saw this pendant.
A Is it worth very much?
B I don't think it's worth an awful lot. It's probably only 9 carat gold. It's got what could be a hallmark on the back of it, but it's really almost worn out now. As far as I remember I paid about £20 for it.
A What's – It's an interesting design. What is it?
B Well, it's called an ankh, and an ankh is a symbol which you often

see in ancient Egyptian tombs, you see it on the walls and wall paintings in tombs, and it was the ancient Egyptian symbol of life. And at the time when I saw it I was just about to have a baby, and it just seemed a good thing to buy in some ways because it did represent life.

11·3 I'm not sure yet

Oh I'm going to, to work as a nurse in, in Africa, in Kenya, and um I'm looking forward to it because it's um such um an exotic country for me.

Well I'd like very much to leave Europe too, you know I've got a cousin in New York I expect I'll go there, maybe I'll find a job.

Well I'll probably get a job in an office first and then perhaps if someone offers me a better job I can I can decide.

Well first I'm going to have a long holiday. I've been very busy lately and I think I need a rest.

Well, my parents have a café, and I expect I will work there for a few months, just to earn some money.

I'm going to write a novel. I've got a very good idea for a best-seller. Well, if you don't mind, I'm not going to tell you the idea, I'd rather keep it as a secret.

12·2 What do you do?

What I do if I have a cold is really just eat as many oranges as I possibly can for the vitamin C, and er take a lot of hot drinks, because I find them very reassuring.

If I can't get to sleep, um I'll try and convince myself that I'm going to sleep by saying in my mind, 'I am going to sleep and I'm going to have a very refreshing long sleep.' But if that doesn't work, then I'll get up and have a, a warm drink and then read, and hope that I'll drop off in the end.

Um the times I've had hiccups, I don't know whether any of these remedies work. Um drinking a lot of water often seems to help, and also um trying to hold your breath for a long time. Um I can do that for quite some time. It doesn't always work but sometimes it helps.

I take as much exercise as I possibly can, and try not to think about it. Because if you start thinking about losing weight you can be sure that you'll eat much more than you normally would. So the thing to do is keep yourself busy and rush around and do as many things as you possibly can. That's how I lose weight.

12·4 All in the mind

Question 1: What is hypochondria?
I think a lot of people get stressed, and when you get stressed you get anxious.

So for example, when you get anxious your heart starts beating faster, and then people notice that their heart's beating faster and they come to believe, 'Maybe I'm having a heart attack.' That makes them even more anxious, and so the heart races even faster. And then if you've got a headache you think, 'Gosh, maybe I've got a brain tumour.' And if you think you've got a brain tumour you get even more tense, and that gives you an even greater headache. And so it goes on.

Question 2: How can you cure hypochondria?
I think one of the things I would do would be to say to this person, 'Look, I think there's a spider crawling up your back,' and I think most people would then say, 'God, I can actually feel this spider crawling up my back, get it off, get it off.' And then at that point I would say, 'No, actually this was a little trick I played on you, there isn't a spider crawling up your back, um what you're actually experiencing are symptoms in your imagination.'

Question 3: Do doctors suffer from hypochondria?
Yes, I think they're probably the worst sufferers of hypochondria. All doctors have been medical students and they go through various blocks of training, so they'll do um, they'll study the diseases of the heart and they'll study the diseases of the brain, and so on. So when they go through and study heart disease most medical students think they've got some heart disease or other, and then when they go through and um study the nervous system most medical students think they've got some brain tumour, and I think it really persists um even once they've, they've qualified.

13·1 Which is better?

A Oh, the Regal's not bad, but I prefer the Metropole.
B Oh really, why's that?
A Well, for one thing it's much quieter, I've found the rooms are more comfortable – I mean, you get more space, and maybe the most important thing, well the staff are more helpful.

A I really like my new job. It's much better than the old one.
B Is it? In what way is it better?
A Well, it's much more interesting than the other job, and it's more convenient – it's closer to home. And the people are much friendlier – they're really nice.

A I don't go to Maxi's Disco any more. The Star's more fun.
B The Star? What's so good about the Star?
A Well, for one thing it's cheaper, and it's got a much livelier atmosphere, and the music is much better.

14·2 Can you tell me the way to ...

Well, you go out of the station, and you come to the main road. Turn left there, go all the way down there, and you come to a T-junction. Turn left there, and then go along that road, you go underneath a bridge – it's the railway bridge. Underneath the railway bridge, and a little bit further on you come to a sort of fork in the road with a garage. Turn sharp left there. And go down that road, I would think about 250 yards, and you'll see it right there on your left – a big building.

When you come out of the station walk straight ahead and very soon you come to the main road – it's the High Street. Turn right, into the High Street, and keep walking down there until you come to the main square, um you'll see that, it's very obvious. At the main square, turn left. Keep on down that road and you'll see a church on the, on the left on a corner. Walk past the church down this same road. Keep on down there – you'll see the river up ahead of you, and just before you get to the river there's a small road off to the left. Go down that road and after a little way there's a bend, quite a definite bend in the road, and just after that bend you'll see it on the right.

Well, as you come out of the station you'll see the High Street in front of you. Turn right onto the High Street and walk along there – keep going straight on and you'll see the main square on your left. And eventually you'll come to Constitution Street in front of you. Now when you come to Constitution Street, turn right, and walk along there for a bit, you'll go over a bridge, a railway bridge. Keep going straight on, and take the first turning on your left – yes, the first turning. You'll see a supermarket on the corner. So, you take this first left, walk down there, and eventually you'll see the building on the right, at the end.

14·4 Los Angeles

Last Christmas I went to Hollywood for two weeks. My best friend was living there. I travelled by plane to Los Angeles, which took thirteen hours, and she picked me up at the airport and drove in her car all the way back to Hollywood. And I was originally rather disappointed, because it all looked rather scruffy. However after I'd recovered from the flight, she started taking me about to see all the wonderful sights. In the first place she lived in a beautiful house up in the mountains, which was a great surprise because that was very beautiful and seemed like a part of another city. She drove me through all the very expensive areas like Belair, where the houses are absolutely enormous. And she took me to Universal Studios, which is where so many of the great old films (and indeed new ones) have been made. We went to Disneyland, which is a little way outside Los Angeles, and spent a whole day there. I didn't think I would enjoy it very much, but I did. And on another day she took me to see a place about 50 miles from Los Angeles, called Santa Barbara, which is a beautiful resort on the beach, and I actually paddled in the Pacific Ocean. And the days flew by, because every day we had an outing. The Americans were terribly polite and friendly, which I liked enormously, and I had a wonderful time.

15·3 Headline news

Police have found the four children from Stonehouse near Glasgow only a few yards away from their homes. They were found in a cellar of an empty building directly across the street from where one of the children lives. Although they were tired, cold and hungry, they are otherwise quite well. It seems that the four were playing in the cellar and somehow managed to lock themselves in. One hundred police and two hundred volunteers joined in the search for the children, but no-one looked in the cellar because they thought it was impossible for the children to get in there. The parents of the four were thrilled that their children were safe, but some neighbours criticised the police for taking so long to find them.

16·1 Leisure activities

Louisa
I enjoy practising the piano, and doing the piano. I have a very good teacher, called Miss Rowe. And I learn the violin, and I enjoy that a lot, and I'm, I've been learning for, I think it's three or four months now. And um I collect shells and rocks, and I've got quite a lot of them. And I go swimming now and again, and I like bike riding.

Carsten
Well, I run a lot in – I live near Epping Forest so I run in the forest. I listen to music, I usually listen to music that I don't or can't play, which is, well it tends to be jazz kind of things. I like cooking – cooking is a hobby of mine, I like cooking for people, really. I've just discovered science fiction reading, I read science fiction books far faster than I read any other kind of books.

Patrick
I spend a lot of my free time going to the theatre to see plays, partly 'cos it's my job to go to the theatre, also because I enjoy it more than just about anything else. Um I read a lot, I read an awful lot of books. I play golf occasionally, when I can, and I have an old house which needs an awful lot of work, so I spend a lot of time decorating, painting the walls, things like that – looking after the house.

Josephine
I'm very interested in languages, because when I go abroad I like to speak with the people there. I try to play the guitar – I don't play very well but every week I meet a friend and we both enjoy ourselves playing together. I live very near the sea. All through the year I go for walks along the shore, and in the summer I go swimming every day. In the winter I like knitting – I make jumpers for my children and my grandchildren, and I enjoy doing different patterns. I spend a lot of time reading, mostly novels, and I'm very fond of poetry – I also write poetry now and then.

16·4 Board games round the world

A OK well this is probably the oldest board game in the world. It's about 5,000 years old, and it was first discovered from drawings in one of the pyramids in Egypt.

B So how do you play it?

A As you can see, we've got a board in the shape of a snake, and we've each got a number of pieces. You've got three pieces in the shape of lions, and I've got three dogs. And the idea is to move our pieces round and round the snake, starting at the tail. And the first person to move all three pieces to the head of the snake is the winner.

B I see, what are the stones for?

A Well, the stones are what we use to move our pieces around the board, and what happens is that you for example if it were your turn, you would take any number of black stones into your hand from one to six, and I have to guess how many stones you're holding. Now if I'm right, I get to move one of my dogs that number of places around the snake. And if I'm wrong, you get to move one of your lions the same number of spaces around the snake. Now there's one other thing. If one of my pieces ends up on the same square as one of your pieces, then your piece has to move back out towards the edge of the snake by one circle, which means that if you're near the beginning of the game then you, you actually go right off the snake and have to start again. And although this is a simple game, in fact when all six pieces are going around the snake it can get quite interesting because people are knocking each other back all the time, and so the guessing becomes, becomes quite, quite important.

B Mm, sounds very good. Shall we have a game?
A Why not?

17·3 Military service

A Does everybody have to do military service in Holland?
B Everybody who's male has to do it, yes, um it's a compulsory national service.
A And you have to go into the army, or can you do other things instead if you like?
B You can, you can um choose to either go into the army, the navy or the air force. Um you can also conscientiously object to going into the army, and you'll have to do another kind of service, which normally means some kind of social service.
A And do most people choose to go into the army?
B Um to my knowledge, yes. Most people see it as 14 months which either happens at the age of 18 or after you've finished your further education.
A What's it like? Is it very hard work?
B Obviously the basic training is fairly hard physical work. Um but from there onwards you can really choose to a certain extent what you want to do, and, um …
A So it could be that you spend your time in an office or in a hospital?
B Yes, very much so. And it's very much a nine to five job, once you've gone through your basic training.
A What about leave? Do you, can you go home?
B Yes, of course. You can actually live, live at home. If you're stationed anywhere near your home you'll just be living at home during your national service.
A Do you find being in the army is a useful experience?
B It is an interesting experience. I'm not sure whether it's useful. It's useful in so far that you learn new skills and you learn to communicate with people, and you learn discipline.

18·3 A working life

Well I studied economics at university, and then I was lucky because I got a job very quickly as an accountant in a local department store. It wasn't exactly what I wanted, but you know it was a first job. I stayed there for four years altogether. After three years I was promoted to accounts manager, er, and I stayed in that job for a year, but then I really got bored, so I decided to leave and I applied for other jobs in the area. But I had no luck getting a second job at all, and I was very short of money, so in the end I had to get a job working as a waitress in a restaurant. Well it wasn't very successful because I'm quite clumsy you see and I kept dropping things, so after a few weeks they gave me the sack. And then, just by chance I met an old friend who I was at university with, and he was working in television. And he got me a job as a television researcher on a programme called 'Business Today'. And after a few months really they decided that they wanted younger presenters of the programme, and I got the job – and I love it.

18·4 Applying for a job

Part 1
A I'm terribly sorry I'm late, I had rather an awkward time finding, finding your office.
B That's quite all right. Please sit down. (Thank you, thank you.) Perhaps now I could start by asking you what kind of work you've been doing at the hotel in Brighton?
A Well, er for the past six months I've been working as a receptionist there, which means that I've been answering the telephone, and generally working at the reception desk, yes.
Part 2
B Now in this hotel we use the Receptel system, which I expect you know is a computerised booking system. Are you familiar with that - would you know how to use it?
A I don't think I would know straight off how to use it. I never have come across that particular kind of booking system. But I have done office work previously and used word processors and various office computers, so I'm quite er quite confident that I could probably learn quite quickly.
Part 3
B Now perhaps you could tell me why you want to leave your present job and join us here?
A Well, I don't, I don't feel that a small private hotel in Brighton really um is what I'm looking for. The hours are very very long and I don't really get paid very much.
B You say the hours are very long. You mean you don't like working long hours?
A Oh no, no, it's not that, it's not that I'm afraid of hard work or anything like that, no, it's, it's very repetitive work, and I don't feel that my qualifications are being properly used.
Part 4
B Now, could I end by asking if you have any questions to ask me?
A Yes. Could you be more specific about what general assistant actually involves?
B It means roughly what it says, really. It's helping out with any day-to-day problems that turn up, not just booking people in and welcoming guests but being, if you like, part of junior management, helping us out day-to-day. We'd expect that.
A I see. And um I'd have holidays, would I?
B You would have holidays, but perhaps we should leave that until you have the job …
… Well, thank you very much for coming along today, and we'll be in touch.
A Thank you, thank you.

19·1 How did it happen?

I was fixing the sink – I was underneath the sink trying to unblock it, and the telephone rang, and I jumped up and banged my head on the sink, so that's why I'm looking a bit like this.

Well I was just cooking the lunch and er the knife slipped and cut my thumb, and I put a plaster on and I thought it was fine, but that was yesterday. Today I woke up and it was enormous.

I was in the park. I was standing by the duck pond, just looking at the ducks, and this kid went by on his skateboard and pushed me in. I'm absolutely wet through and very cold.

20·1 Familiar faces

He had, he had a, a very big moustache, I think that's the main feature about him, and thick wiry hair, and probably quite a stout man, quite fat, I think – um not tall, medium, medium-sized, quite stout, yeah.

He was very tall. He looked very thin and a face as if it had been carved out. Um curly hair, a very large nose, and a moustache and beard, um which made him look um very, very hard.

20·3 Character sketch

A Chris, (Mm?) I'm dying for a cup of tea. I don't suppose you could, you could lend me 50p, could you?
B Of course, of course I'll lend you 50p. (Oh thanks.) Look, 50p's not much good – why don't you er – look, why don't you have £5, that'll keep you going all day. (Oh.) You can pay me back whenever you want, doesn't matter.
A Oh thanks, thanks very much. (All right?)
A Hello. (Hi.) Gosh, it's very hot and crowded in here, isn't it?
B Yes, it is a bit.
A Um, my name's Anne. (Oh, um.) What's yours?
B Ch- Chris.
A Chris. Hi.
B Hi.

A Excuse me, I say, (Yeah), sorry, but you just dropped this £10 note.
B What? Oh, oh, oh oh thank you, oh dear, oh thank you very much.
A That's all right. Just – I should put it in your purse if I were you.
B Oh yeah oh dear, wait a minute, where's my – oh here we are, yes. (All right?) Yes. Yes, thanks very much. (OK.) Bye.

20·4 The Dream Game

All right, you're in a dream, you're asleep and you're dreaming, and in your dream you find yourself in your ideal house – the house you'd really love to live in. Now, close your eyes, and try to imagine the house. What can you say about it?

All right, you leave the house, and you find yourself on a path, and while you're walking along this path you see a cup on the ground. Imagine the cup. What sort of cup is it?

Now you're in some woods, walking through the woods, and you come to a clearing where there aren't any trees or anything around. In the middle of the clearing there's a building. What sort of building is it?

There's a garden all around. Have a think about the garden. Tell me about it.

All right, so you walk out of the garden and finish walking through the wood, and suddenly in front of you, you see a wall. Now the wall is too high to climb over and too long to walk round. But a small door opens in the wall. Are you going to go through it?

Well on the other side is water. What sort of water is it? Do you want to swim in it, for instance?

All right thank you. That's all.

21·4 What's going to happen?

In this one, the, the gunfighter is going to, to walk towards those four men, and they're going to walk a little towards him. And then he's going to draw his gun first, and he's probably going to shoot two or three of the, of the other gun fighters. But in the end I think they're going to kill him.

In this one, the waiter's going to come and he's going to give him the bill, and then this man's going to discover that he hasn't got his cheque book or wallet, and um he's not going to be able to pay. So there'll be a big argument, and um either the waiter will make him wash the dishes, but I think, I think the woman is going to help the man, I think she's actually going to, to pay the bill for him.

22·1 Where in the world?

I come from, from Germany, from, from the Black Forest, that is in the south west of West Germany. It's quite close to the Swiss border and the French border, and um it's a mountainous area, quite high mountains, in fact. There are a lot of forests, as the name suggests, um we have beautiful valleys and lakes, where a lot of people go walking in summer and skiing in winter – it's, it's quite a famous tourist area in in Germany.

I come from Indonesia, and I was born in West Sumatra. West Sumatra is one of the islands in Indonesia. It consists of mountains, there are a lot of forests there, and there are a lot of wild animals we still can find there. West Sumatra has got interesting places to visit. If you go to the lake, we call this Maninjau Lakes, it is a big lake and it's very lovely.

I come from the Hague in Holland. It's actually the centre of Dutch government, Dutch parliament is based there. Um in its surrounding areas there is a lot of agricultural land. Um knowing Holland it's fairly flat and also is actually below the sea level. It's ringed by canals and not so much windmills any more but pumping stations to actually keep the water from the land.

Auckland's the biggest city in New Zealand. It's situated between two harbours – beautiful harbours, one comes in from the Pacific Ocean on the eastern side and the other one comes in from the west coast, from the Tasman Sea. So the city's between those two harbours and it's built on some extinct volcanoes, about seven or eight of them, I think. It's very green, there's lots of lovely beaches, and lots of islands in the harbour and just outside of it, so boating's a very popular sport.

I come from Aden, the capital of the People's Democratic Republic of Yemen. Aden is the capital of the country. The country surrounding Aden consists mainly of farmland. This is up to a distance of about 40 km, and sometimes more. But then after that there are some deserts to the east of the er, of the capital. There we can find some minerals like oil.

22·4 Car chaos

In some places they ban cars from city centres altogether. In Florence in Italy for instance the whole of the city is for pedestrians only from 7.30 in the morning until 6.30 in the evening.

Another idea is to make people pay if they want to bring their cars into the city centre. They do this in Singapore. They have checkpoints around the centre and if you're bringing your car in you can be stopped and if you've got less than four people in it then you have to pay.

The Netherlands is one place which is particularly keen on this idea, being such a flat country. There are now 14,000 km of cycle paths there, so you can go more or less anywhere by bike.

In Britain in some cities they're using er what they call a Park and Ride scheme. They build big car parks on the outskirts of the city and you park your car there and then there's a bus which takes you into the city, you do your shopping, whatever, get the bus back again to your car.

In Portland Oregon in the United States they decided not to build a new motorway at all, and instead they used the money to improve bus services and build a new railway. So now most people leave their cars at home and use public transport instead.

In Hong Kong, for example, there's a computer-based system which tracks cars' movements in the city centre and drivers are billed monthly according to when and how often they've driven into the city centre.

23·4 Murder in the office

Mr Green
Well I um stayed in the office until just before 10 and then I went out to meet an old friend of mine. Um there was no-one in the office when I left, except Miss Brown my secretary of course, and I er – I came back about 15 minutes ago. Er, Mrs White and Mr Black were already here, and I went through into my own office and er – and that was when I found my wife.

Mrs White
I was here from 9 till 9.45, and then I went out for a meeting at the bank. I stayed out for about an hour, I suppose. I met Mr Black as I was coming up the stairs, and Mr Green came in just after me. The secretary wasn't there. She only came back a few minutes ago.

Miss Brown
I was in the office until about 10. There was no-one else there except Mr Green, who was in his own office. Um at 10 o'clock Mrs Green arrived. She hadn't made an appointment, but I showed her into Mr Green's office of course. I thought he was a bit surprised to see her. Anyway, then I left the office to buy some coffee and to go to the post office, and I've only just got back.

Mr Black
Well I've been out of the office all morning. At 10 o'clock I had a meeting with some customers at the Sheraton. I saw Mr Green there too, as it happens. He was sitting at a table having coffee with a woman. I've only been back for about 20 minutes. I met Mrs White on the stairs and we came in together.

Reference section

1 Description

There is/are

- We use *there is* with singular nouns.
  We use *there are* with plural nouns. Before plural nouns we often use *some* (positive sentences) and *any* (negative sentences). (See also Unit 9.)

- Positive and negative forms:

There's There isn't	a lemon	in the fridge.
There are some eggs		
There aren't any eggs		

- Yes/no questions + short answers:

Is there a lemon	in the fridge?	Yes, there is. No, there isn't.
Are there any eggs		Yes, there are. No, there aren't.

have/has got

- *has got* is similar in meaning to *there is/are*:
  The house *has got*   =   There's a bathroom
  a bathroom.   in the house.

- Positive and negative forms:

The hotel	has got hasn't got	balconies.
The rooms	have got haven't got	

- Yes/no questions + short answers:

Has the hotel got	balconies?	Yes, it has. No, it hasn't.
Have the rooms got		Yes, they have. No, they haven't.

- As well as *have/has got*, we can use *have/has*:
  The hotel *has* 30 rooms. The rooms *have* balconies. This is more common in written English.

Place prepositions

I live	next to / opposite / near a bank. between a bookshop and a café. in North Street.

There's a car park	behind / in front of the station.

2 Family and friends

Family relations

Male	Female	Common
father	mother	parent(s)
brother	sister	–
son	daughter	child(ren)
grandfather	grandmother	grandparent(s)
grandson	granddaughter	grandchild(ren)
uncle	aunt	–
nephew	niece	–
–	–	cousin(s)

- There are two general words for 'people in your family': *relatives* and *relations*.
- Relations by marriage – add *-in-law*:
  father-in-law (= your husband's/wife's father)
  sister-in-law (= your husband's/wife's sister)
- English has no common word meaning 'brothers and sisters', so we say, for example, 'How many brothers and sisters have you got?'
- English has no special words for male and female cousins.

Other people

- *neighbours* = people who live near you.
  next-door neighbours = people who live next door.
- *flat-mate* = someone who shares your flat.
  room-mate = someone who shares your room.
- My *boyfriend/girlfriend* = the person I'm *going out with*.
  For other friends say 'a friend of mine', 'one of my friends'.

Personal relationships

Action verbs	State verbs
meet / get to know	know
get engaged (to)	be engaged (to)
get married (to)	be married (to)
get divorced (from)	be divorced (from)

- Noun forms: *engagement, marriage, divorce*.
  wedding = the marriage ceremony: 'I hope they invite me to their wedding.'
- If you're not married, you're *single*.

3 Habits, customs and facts

Present simple tense

- We use the Present simple tense to talk about:
  - repeated or habitual actions (habits, customs, lifestyles):
    I *get up* at 6 every morning.
    Most people *send* birthday cards.
  - present states, attitudes and feelings:
    She *lives* in New York.
    I *like* ice-cream.
  - facts (things that are generally true):
    Penguins *eat* fish.
    Many Canadians *speak* French.
- Positive and negative forms:

I You We They	live don't live	in London.
He She	lives doesn't live	

- Yes/no questions + short answers:

Do	you they	drive?	Yes, I do. No, they don't.
Does	he she		Yes, he does. No, she doesn't.

- *Wh-* questions:

What	do	you they	do in the evenings?
	does	he she	

Frequency adverbs

always often/usually sometimes not often / not usually only never

- The normal position of these adverbs is before the main verb:

She	often goes doesn't often go	to the theatre.

- *only*:
  They *only* see each other at weekends.
  I *only* smoke in the evening.
- *often* and *usually* are slightly different in meaning:
  They *often* eat out. (= They eat out a lot.)
  They *usually* eat out. (= They eat out most of the time.)

4 Going places

Vehicles, people and places

bus	driver	bus station
train	driver	station
plane	pilot, steward(ess)	airport
boat, ship	captain, sailor	port, harbour
car	driver	garage
bicycle (bike)	cyclist, rider	–
motorcycle (motorbike)	motorcyclist, rider	–

- Other people in a car, train, etc., are *passengers*.
- You *drive* a car. You *ride* a bike, a motorbike, or a horse.
- You get *in / out of* a car or taxi. You get *on/off* a bus, train, bike.
- You go somewhere *by* bus, plane, train, etc.
  If you walk, you go *on foot*.
- If you get to the station *in time* (= early enough), you'll *catch* the train. If you're *late*, you'll *miss* it. The train should arrive *on time* (= at the correct time).

Describing public transport

- Opposite pairs of adjectives:

comfortable	uncomfortable
cheap	expensive
fast	slow
safe	dangerous
empty	crowded
reliable	unreliable

Travel information

- The train *leaves* Paris at 8.30.

It	*arrives in/at* *reaches* *gets to*	Berlin at 5.00.

- Questions and answers:
  - How can I get to London?
  - (You can get there) by bus.
  - How long does it take?
  - (It takes) 5 hours.
  - How much does it cost?
  - (It costs) £25.

5 Now

Present continuous tense

- We use the Present continuous tense to talk about:
  - things happening 'now', at the moment of speaking:
    Shh! I'*m reading* the newspaper.
    Look – they'*re coming* towards us.
  - current activities, things happening 'around now':
    He'*s learning* to play the piano.
    She'*s studying* hard for her exams.
- Compare Present continuous and simple:
  - She *lives* in Amsterdam (= in general, it's her home) but she'*s staying* with friends in Berlin (= just at the moment).
  - I *work* in a bank (= in general) but I'*m looking* for a new job (= around now, during the present period).
- Positive and negative forms:

I	'm 'm not	
You We They	're 're not	having lunch.
He She	's 's not	

Note that *are* and *is* have two possible negative short forms:
You're → You *aren't* or You'*re not*
He's → He *isn't* or He'*s not*

- Yes/no questions + short answers:

Are	you they	coming?	Yes, I am. No, I'm not.
			Yes, we/they are. No, we/they aren't.
Is	he she		Yes he/she is. No, he/she isn't.

- Wh- questions:

Where	are	you they	staying at the moment?
	is	he she	

There is/are + -ing

There's a woman There are some people	waiting outside.

6 Food and drink

Types of food

Type	Examples	Shops
fruit	apple, orange, banana	greengrocer
vegetables	cabbage, onion, carrot	greengrocer
meat	lamb, chicken, beef	butcher
fish	cod, herring, tuna	fish shop / fishmonger

- You buy other food (e.g. *coffee, rice, flour, eggs, salt*) at a *grocer's*, a *general store*, or a *supermarket*.
- You can also buy food from *stalls* at a *market*.
- Many words for food (e.g. *sugar, meat, fruit, cheese, bread*) are non-count nouns – they are not usually used in the plural form:
  Would you like some fruit?
  Fish is good for you.
  (For count and non-count nouns, see Unit 9.)
- Note these common expressions with *of*:
  a kilo of apples   a litre of oil
  a loaf of bread   a packet of tea
  a bag of sugar   a tin/can of soup

Meals and dishes

- Meals: *breakfast, lunch, dinner, supper*.
- Meals sometimes have several courses:
  starter, main course, dessert or *sweet*.
- Describing dishes:
  It's a stew. It's *made from* meat and onions.
  It'*s got* rice *in it*.
  You *serve* it *with* cream.

At a restaurant

- You sometimes *reserve/book* a table.
  You *order* food / a meal / a drink.
  The waiter *serves* the food.
  At the end you *pay the bill*.
- Asking for things:
  Could you bring me a knife?
  Could I have the bill, please?
  I'*d like* some more coffee, please.
  I'*ll have* chicken and chips, please.
- Offers:
  Would you like a drink?

7 The past

Past simple tense

- We use the Past simple tense to talk about:
  - single events in the past:
    They *arrived* on Saturday.
    He *met* her in 1944.
  - past states
    When I *was* a child, I *lived* in Australia.
  - repeated events in the past:
    My father *took* me to school every day.

- Positive and negative forms:

I You He She We They	liked didn't like saw didn't see	the film.

- Yes/no questions + short answers:

Did	you they he she	go out?

| Yes, | I/we
they
he
she | did. |
| No, | | didn't. |

- Wh- questions:

When	did	you they he she	leave school?

Past time expressions

- Prepositions:
  - *at* for points of time, including expressions with *end*:
    at 6 o'clock, *at* the weekend, *at* the end of the month
  - *on* for days and dates:
    on Monday, *on* 15th May
  - *in* for other periods of time:
    in June, *in* 1980
- We don't use a preposition:
  - with *last*:
    last Tuesday, *last* year
  - with the phrases:
    today, *yesterday*, *the day before yesterday*
- We use *ago* to measure time back from now:

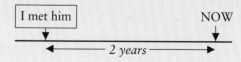

I met him *two years ago*.

8 Somewhere to live

Kinds of home

- They live in a *house, flat/apartment, cottage, block of flats / apartment block*.
  (British English: *flat*; US English: *apartment*)
- Their flat is on the third floor. →
  It's a third-floor flat.
- Their apartment's got five rooms. →
  It's a five-room apartment.

Position and outlook

- Their house is
  in the town centre / the suburbs / the country.
  on a main road / a square.
  near the town centre / the sea / the airport.
- Our apartment
  has a view of the park.
  looks out on the park.
  faces north/south/east/west.

Rooms and furniture

Room	Typical furniture
living room	armchair, sofa, carpet, curtains, TV
kitchen	cooker, fridge, cupboards, shelves, sink
bathroom	bath, shower, mirror, washbasin
study	desk, table, chair, bookshelf
bedroom	(double/single) bed, wardrobe

- *living room* and *sitting room* mean the same.
- *fridge = refrigerator*.
- Note the irregular plural: *shelf* → *shelves*.
- The word *furniture* is non-count, so it has no plural:
  We need some new furniture.
  (See Unit 9.)
- Most houses and flats have a *hall* (by the front door) and a *toilet*; some have *balconies*.
  Houses usually have *stairs*, and a front or back *garden*.

Describing rooms

- Adjectives:
  bare, empty, cluttered;
  tidy, untidy;
  clean, dirty;
  plain, colourful;
  comfortable, uncomfortable, cosy.

- The room needs | a new carpet.
  | more furniture.

- It needs | cleaning.
  | painting.
  | tidying.

9 Quantity

Count and non-count nouns

Count	Non-count
a book, books an apple, apples a room, rooms	money sugar furniture

- Count nouns have a singular and a plural form. In the singular we can use an indefinite article (*a/an*).
- Non-count (or 'mass') nouns have no plural form and no indefinite article.

some & any

Count	Non-count
I've got some books. I haven't got any books. Have you got any books?	I've got some money. I haven't got any money. Have you got any money?

- We use *some* and *any* with non-count nouns (*some money*) and with plurals (*some books*).
- In general, we use *some* in positive sentences, and *any* in negatives and questions.

Quantity expressions

- Positive and negative forms:

He's got	a lot of too much	money.
	a lot of too many	friends.

He hasn't got	much money.
	many friends.

- Question forms:

Has he got	much money?
	many friends?

How much money	has he got?
How many friends	

- We use *much* with non-count nouns, *many* with count nouns.
- In positive sentences, we usually say *a lot of* (or *lots of*) instead of *much/many*.
- *Too much/many* has a negative meaning:
  He's got *a lot of* money. (probably good)
  He's got *too much* money. (probably bad – he doesn't know what to do with it)
- *not enough* is opposite in meaning to *too much / many*. We use it with count and non-count nouns:

He hasn't got enough	money.
	friends.

10 Clothes

Names of clothes

HEAD/NECK	hat, scarf	
BODY	shirt/blouse, teeshirt jumper/pullover, jacket	suit dress
LEGS	skirt, trousers, jeans, shorts tights, stockings	coat pyjamas
FEET	socks, shoes, boots, sandals	

- *clothes* is a general word – it is only used in the plural:
  He likes wearing smart clothes.
- *trousers*, *jeans*, *tights*, *pyjamas* only have a plural form, but we can say '*a pair of* trousers', etc.
- Other common 'pairs':
  a pair of shoes, a pair of socks, a pair of glasses.
- Jewellery:
  necklace (round your neck)
  earrings (on your ears)
  bracelet (round your arm)
  ring (on your finger)

Materials and patterns

- It's made of *cotton/wool/leather/nylon*.
- It's *striped/plain*.
  It has a *check pattern* / a *flowery pattern*.

Verbs

Transitive	Intransitive
put on + noun take off + noun change + noun	dress, get dressed undress, get undressed change, get changed

- In the morning I *get dressed*. I *put on* a suit.

He	*took off* his clothes *undressed*	and jumped in the water.

  She *changed* her clothes. She *changed out of* her dress and *into* a pair of jeans.

Buying clothes

- That jacket *suits* you. (= it looks good on you)
  It *goes with* your trousers. (= they look good together)
- Is it *small*, *medium* or *large*? What *size* is it?
  It's *size* 14.
  Try it on and see if it *fits*. (= it's the right size)
- How much does it *cost*?

11 Future plans

going to

- We use *going to* to talk about intentions or plans (things we have decided to do).

- Positive and negative forms:

I	'm / 'm not		stay at home.
You We They	're / 're not	going to	
He She	's / 's not		have a party.

- Question forms:

Are	you they	going to	stay at home?
Is	he she		have a party?

What	are	you they	going to do?
	is	he she	

Present continuous tense

- We use the Present continuous for things that are <u>definitely arranged</u> in the future. Compare:
  - We're *going to* have a party. (= We've decided to have one.)
  - We're *having* a party. (= It's all arranged – we've invited the people already.)
- With the verbs *go* and *come*, we often use the Present continuous instead of *going to* to avoid 'going to go' and 'going to come':
  Are you *coming* to the wedding?
  We're *going* swimming tomorrow.

will

- We use *will* to talk about things we are not yet sure about (we haven't decided yet). We usually add *I expect* or *probably*:
  When I leave college *I'll probably* go abroad.
  I expect we'll stay at home this weekend.
- We also use *will* to make predictions. (See Unit 21.)

Future time expressions

- *in* is used to measure time 'into the future':
  She's leaving school *in* three weeks. (= 3 weeks from now)
- no preposition:
  - phrases with *this* and *next*:
    this week, next Tuesday, next year
  - the phrases:
    tomorrow, the day after tomorrow

12 How do you feel?

Aches and pains

noun	pain ache	I've got *a pain* in my knee. I've got *a backache*.
verb	ache hurt	My back *aches*. My knee *hurts*.
adjective	sore	My knee feels *sore*. I've got a *sore* throat.

- An *ache* is a continuous pain. We usually write *toothache*, *backache* and *headache* as one word (but *stomach ache* as two).
- *sore* = it hurts when you touch it.

Illnesses

- With most illnesses, we use *have* or *have got*:
  He has a cold every winter. (= repeated)
  He's got a bad cold. (= now)
  In the past we use *had*:
  He had a bad cold last week.
- Other common expressions:
  have a cough, have a headache, have 'flu, have a temperature (= more than 37°)
- You can also *catch* a cold, and *give* it to other people.
- You feel *ill* = you don't feel well, there's something wrong with you.
  You feel *sick* = you want to *be sick* (perhaps you've eaten too much chocolate).
  In U.S. English, *sick* can have either meaning.

Going to the doctor

- If you *fall* (= become) *ill*, you may *make an appointment* to see the doctor.
- He/she will ask you questions and *examine* you.
- Then he/she'll probably write you a *prescription*. You take it to the *chemist's* (or the *pharmacy*), and they'll give you some *medicine*.
- When you get home, you *take* the medicine. If you're lucky, you'll soon *get better / recover*.

13 Comparison

Comparative and superlative adjectives

- Adjectives with one syllable add -er, -est:
  short, shorter, shortest
- Adjectives with three or more syllables add more, most:
  beautiful, more beautiful, most beautiful
- Adjectives with two syllables may follow either pattern, so you should learn them individually. But:
  - those ending in -ly always add -er, -est
    friendly, friendlier, friendliest
  - those ending in -ful always add more, most
    careful, more careful, most careful

- Irregular forms:

Adjective	Comparative	Superlative
good	better	best
bad	worse	worst
much/many	more	most
little	less	least
far	farther/	farthest/
	further	furthest

Comparative structures

	younger shorter tidier cleverer more active more intelligent	than	my brother. you. the rest of my family.
I'm			

Which	is bigger, has a bigger population,	London or Tokyo?

Superlative structures

	youngest shortest tidiest cleverest most active most intelligent	person in my family.
I'm the		

14 About town

Places in town

Activity	Typical places
shopping	shop, department store, market
eating/drinking	restaurant, café, pub
entertainment	theatre, cinema, concert hall
sport	stadium, sports centre, park, swimming pool
religion	church, mosque, temple, synagogue
sightseeing	art gallery, museum, palace, castle
nightlife	disco(thèque), night club, bar

- go + -ing: go swimming, sightseeing, shopping
  go for: go for a swim, for a walk, for a meal
  go to: go to the theatre, the cinema, the shops
          go to a concert, a café; go to church
- With most of these places, we can use at or in:
  She's at the theatre. (= seeing a play)
  She's in the theatre. (= in the theatre building)

Street directions

- Asking the way:

  Excuse me, | can you tell me the way to ...?
              | how can I get to ...?

- Giving directions:
  Go (straight) along this road.
  Turn left/right at the (traffic lights).
  Go on until you get to (the main road).
  You'll see it on your left/right.

- Prepositions:

  down/up/along the road

  across the road

  past the church

  over the bridge

  under the bridge

Opposite adjectives

quiet	–	noisy
quiet	–	busy
clean	–	dirty
beautiful	–	ugly
lively	–	dull
interesting	–	boring
friendly	–	unfriendly

15 Past and present

Present perfect tense

- We use the Present perfect tense to talk about:
  - recent events, news:
    We've just *had* a baby.
    They've *found* the missing children.
  - changes that have taken place (what is different now from before):
    They've *moved* to Wales. (= now they live there)
    She's *found* a new job.
  - personal experiences:
    I've never *ridden* a horse
    He's *been* to Hong Kong several times.
- We can often express the same idea using either the Present perfect tense (*what has happened*) or the Present tense (*how things are now*):
  He has woken up. (= He is awake now.)
  They've gone abroad. (= They live abroad now.)
- We use the Present perfect tense when we're not interested in *when* things happened, but only in *the fact that* they've happened. If we focus on *when*, *where* or *how*, we use the Past simple:
  They've *moved* to Wales. They *went* there a few months ago.
  - *Have* you *eaten* raw fish? (= at any time)
  - Yes. I *tried* it once last year. It *was* delicious.
- Positive and negative forms:

I You	've (have) haven't	washed the dishes. had a haircut. bought a new watch.
He She	's (has) hasn't	

- Yes/no questions + short answers:

Have	you they	finished?	Yes, I have. No, they haven't.
Has	he she		Yes, he has. No, she hasn't.

- *Wh-* questions:

Where	have	you they	been?
	has	he she	

- *have gone to* and *have been to*:
  - They've *gone to* the cinema. (They're in the cinema now.)
  - They've *been to* the cinema. (They've come back home again now.)

16 Free time

Leisure activities

SPORTS/GAMES	football, tennis, motor racing, athletics; chess, cards
OTHER OUTDOOR ACTIVITIES	walking, cycling, fishing, skiing, horse-riding
OTHER INDOOR ACTIVITIES	cooking, reading, knitting, stamp collecting, flower arranging

- *Go + -ing*:
  swim → go swimming
  cycle → go cycling
  fish → go fishing
- *Play*: You can play *games* and *musical instruments*.
  Games: play football, cards
  Musical instruments: play *the* piano, *the* guitar
- *Do*:
  She *does* a lot of reading. (= She reads a lot.)
  I *don't do* much walking. (= I don't walk much.)

Enjoyment and skill

- *Like/enjoy + -ing* or noun:

I	like enjoy	reading. (playing) golf. going to the theatre.

- He *can* play the guitar.
  I *know how to* knit. (= I can do it.)
  She's *good at* swimming. (= She swims well.)

Sports: games and races

- Some sports and how they are played:

Sport	People	Verb	Equipment
football	teams	kick	ball, goal
basketball	teams	throw	ball, basket
tennis	players	hit	ball, racquet, net
golf	players	hit	ball, club, hole

- You can *win* games and races, or you can *lose* them.
  If you win, you *beat* the other player(s).
- You win games by *scoring* points or goals.
  You win races by finishing in the fastest time.

17 Obligation

Obligation and lack of obligation

must have to	mustn't can't
can	don't have to

- *must* and *have to* mean almost the same. We usually use *must* when we tell people what to do:
  - Doctor to patient: You *must* stay in bed.
  We usually use *have to* when we talk <u>about</u> obligation:
  - One patient to another: I *have to* stay in bed.
- *mustn't* and *can't* mean 'don't do this':

  You | *mustn't*
can't | cross now – the light's red.

- *don't have to* means 'it isn't necessary':
  You *don't have to* pay to get in – it's free.
- *must* and *mustn't*, *can* and *can't* are modal verbs. They are followed by infinitive without 'to':

You She We They	must mustn't can can't	go.

- Question forms:

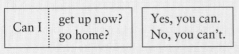

Can I	get up now? go home?		Yes, you can. No, you can't.

Do I have to	get up now? go home?	Yes, you do. No, you don't.

should & ought to

- We use *should* and *ought to*:
  - to express disapproval:
    She *ought to* write to her parents more often.
    You *shouldn't* smoke so much.
  - to give advice:
    You *ought to* see a doctor.
    You *should* ask him what the problem is.
- *should* is followed by infinitive without *to*.
  ought is followed by *to* + infinitive.

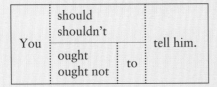

You	should shouldn't		tell him.
	ought ought not	to	

18 A day's work

Places and jobs

Places	Typical jobs
hospital	doctor, nurse
office	manager, accountant, secretary, typist
restaurant	waiter/waitress, chef/cook
hotel	manager, receptionist, porter
nightclub	singer, pianist, disc jockey
buildings	builder, painter, plumber, cleaner
the street	policeman/policewoman (police officer), postman/postwoman, bus driver
theatre	actor/actress, director
garage	mechanic

- General words:
  in an office: *employee*
  in a factory: *worker*
  in a shop: *assistant*
- *-er* ending: *driver, waiter, porter, builder*
  -or ending: *actor, director, doctor*
  -ist ending: *pianist, receptionist, typist*
- male/female pairs: *waiter/waitress, actor/actress, policeman/policewoman, postman/postwoman*

Talking about work

- Questions:
  What's your job?
  What do you do?
  Where do you work?
  How much do you earn?
- I work *in* a bank / *in* a hospital;
  for a large company / *for* Esso.
- I'm *self-employed*. (= I work for myself.)
  I'm *unemployed*. (= I haven't got a job.)
- I *deal with* the accounts/customers.
  I *look after* small children.
  I *mend/repair* cars/clocks.

Careers

- When you leave school or university, you *apply for* a job.
  If you're lucky, you'll *get* the job.
  After some time, you may be *promoted*.
  If you're unlucky, you may *get the sack*. (= *lose* your job)
  Or you may decide to *leave* your job and *find* another one.
  When you're 65 you'll probably *retire*.

19 Narration

Past continuous tense

- We use the Past continuous tense to talk about:
  - the background to events in the past (things that were going on at the time):
  He *was having* a shower when someone knocked at the door.
  While I *was climbing* over a wall, I slipped and hurt my knee.
  - scenes in the past:
  The street was full of people. They *were shouting* and *singing*.

- Positive and negative forms:

I He She	was wasn't	listening.
We You They	were weren't	

- Yes/no questions + short answers:

Were	you they	eating?	Yes, I/he/she was. No, I/he/she wasn't.
Was	he she		Yes, we/they were. No, we/they weren't.

- *Wh-* questions:

Why	were	you they	asking questions?
	was	he she	

when & while

- *when/while* + Past continuous:

When While	I was having supper, someone phoned.

Someone phoned	*when* *while*	I was having supper.

- *when* + Past simple:
  I was having supper *when* someone phoned.

Describing scenes

- *There was/were* + *-ing*:

There was a man There were two men	sitting in the corner.

- Other phrases with *-ing*:
  They were sitting at a table, *playing* cards.
  There were some children running around in the street, *kicking* a ball.

20 People

Physical appearance

- What does he/she look like?

GENERAL	tall, short, medium height; fat, thin, slim
FACE	long, thin, wide, broad
SKIN	fair, dark(-skinned)
HAIR	thick, thin; long, short; wavy, curly, straight; fair/blond, dark

- Other features:
  He has a *beard* / a *moustache*.
  He's *bald*. (= he has no hair)
  He/She has *glasses*, *earrings*.
- *slim* is a polite word for *thin*.
- Word order:
  We use adjectives in the order shown in the table:
  She's tall and slim, with long wavy dark hair.
  He's medium height, and has a long thin face and a beard.
  She has a wide face and short fair hair.

Age

- How old is he/she?

He's	in	his	(early) (mid) (late)	twenties. fifties.
She's		her		

- He's in his *teens*. / He's a *teenager*. (= between 13 and 19)
  She's *middle-aged*. (= between 40 and 60)
  He's *elderly*. (= over 70)

Character adjectives

- What's he/she like? What kind of person is he/she?
  Opposite pairs:

Positive	Negative
generous	mean
honest	dishonest
friendly	unfriendly
hard-working	lazy
good-tempered	bad-tempered
patient	impatient
unselfish	selfish

21 Prediction

will, won't & might

- We use *will*, *won't* and *might*:
  - to make predictions:
    You *will* meet a tall dark stranger.
    It *might* rain tomorrow.
  - to tell people what to expect when they are about to do something:
    It *won't* hurt.
    They*'ll* ask you for your passport.

- Degrees of probability:

Food prices	will (probably) might (probably) won't	go up.

might = perhaps they will.
probably comes <u>after</u> *will* but <u>before</u> *won't*.

- Yes/no questions + short answers:

Will	they win? he come soon? it hurt?	Yes, they will. He might. No, it won't.

- *Wh-* questions:

What will they ask me? When will the letter arrive? How will I recognise you?

First conditional structures (if & unless)

If	we hurry	we'll get there on time.
Unless		we'll be late.

- After *if/unless*, we use the Present simple tense, although we are talking about the future.
- *Unless* means *if* + *don't/doesn't*:
  - *Unless* you leave now, you'll miss the bus. (= If you don't leave now ...)
  - I won't pay them *unless* they work harder (= I'll only pay them if they work harder; if they don't work harder, I won't pay them.)

going to

- We use *going to* for predictions when we can already see the signs of something happening, or when things have already started to happen:
  Look – it's *going to* rain. (I can see black clouds.)
  I think I'm *going to* be sick. (I have a funny feeling in my stomach.)
- The main use of *going to* is for expressing intention. (See Unit 11.)

22 Around the world

Geographical features

- hill, mountain, volcano, plain, valley
  lake, river, estuary (= mouth of a river), sea, ocean
  coast, beach, island
  forest, desert, farmland, prairie (= grassland)
- The town is *in* the mountains.
  on a lake/river.
  on the coast / the sea.
  on the border.
  on the edge of a desert.
  in the north/south/east/west of the country

Climate

Nouns	Adjectives	Sentences
rain	rainy	It's raining.
snow	snowy	It's snowing.
wind	windy	The wind's blowing.
sun	sunny	The sun's shining.
cloud	cloudy	–

- *climate* = the weather in general.
- Other adjectives: *hot, warm, cool, cold; dry, wet, humid* (= the air is damp).
- Some countries have four *seasons*:
  spring, summer, autumn, winter.
  Some countries have a *dry season* and a *wet* (or *rainy*) *season*.

Countries and nationalities

	Country	Nationality
-ish	Spain Poland	Spanish Polish
-an	Russia Iran	Russian Iranian
-ese	China Japan	Chinese Japanese
-i	Pakistan Somalia	Pakistani Somali

- Some irregular forms:
  The Netherlands – Dutch   Greece – Greek
  Switzerland – Swiss   France – French
  Norway – Norwegian   Wales – Welsh
  Portugal – Portuguese   Denmark – Danish
- Some nationalities have different noun forms for *people*; for example:
  He's French. = He's a Frenchman.
  She's Turkish. = She's a Turk.
  He's Spanish. = He's a Spaniard.
  She's Scottish. = She's a Scot.
- Syria, Egypt and Libya are all *Arab* countries. People there speak *Arabic*.

23 Duration

Present perfect continuous tense

- We use the Present perfect continuous tense to talk about events that started in the past and are still going on now:
  They*'ve been living* here since 1960. (= They came here in 1960, and they're still here.)
  I*'ve been waiting* for two hours. (= I started waiting two hours ago, and I'm still waiting.)

- Positive and negative forms:

I We You They	've (have) haven't	been	waiting.
He She	's (has) hasn't		

- *Wh-* questions:

How long	have	you they	been	learning English?
	has	he she		

for & since

- *for* is used with periods of time.
  since is used with points of time.

I've been waiting	for	half an hour. three months. a long time.
	since	9 o'clock. last Tuesday. January 1st.

- We can also use *for* with other tenses:
  I stayed there *for* a year.
  I'm going on holiday *for* a week.

Non-continuous forms

- Some verbs are not normally used in the continuous form (they are called *stative verbs*). The most common are *be*, *know* and *have* (= possess). With these verbs, we use the Present perfect *simple* instead of Present perfect continuous:
  I*'ve known* them for three months.
  She*'s been* awake since six o'clock.
  He*'s had* that jacket for years.

- With some verbs (e.g. *live*, *work*, *stay*, *feel*) we can use either the simple or continuous form with no great difference in meaning:

He's	*worked* *been working*	in that office for 30 years.

24 But is it art?

Artists and their work

Art forms	People
stories, novels	author, writer, novelist
poetry, poems	poet
plays	playwright
films	director
painting	painter, artist
sculpture	sculptor
music	composer

- *Art* and *artist* are general words, but are often used to talk about painting:
  Botticelli was a great Renaissance *artist*.

Places

You go to see/hear ...	at a/an ...
paintings/sculpture	art gallery, museum
music	concert hall
plays	theatre
opera	opera house
films	cinema

- You go to an art gallery to see an *exhibition* of paintings.
  You go to a concert hall to hear a *concert*.

Performers

- People involved in plays and films:
  director, *producer*, *actors*, *stars*.
- Classical music is often performed by a *conductor* and an *orchestra*.
  Popular music is often performed by a *pop/rock singer* with a *band* (or *group*).

At home

- You can watch films, plays, etc., *on TV* or *on video*.
  You can listen to music, plays, etc., *on the radio*.
  You can listen to music on a *record* (LP), a *cassette* or a *compact disc* (CD).

Literature

- Forms of literature: *novel*, *short story*, *poem*, *play*.
- Some popular types of novel: *thrillers*, *detective stories*, *science fiction*, *romantic novels*.
- Children (and some adults) read *comics / comic strips*.
- Most books are sold in *paperback* editions. The *cover* tells you the *title*, the name of the *author* and the *publisher*.

Modal verbs

Structures with modal verbs

• Positive and negative forms:

will ('ll)	won't
shall ('ll)	shan't
can	can't (cannot)
must	mustn't
may	may not
might	might not
would	wouldn't
should	shouldn't
could	couldn't

• Modal verbs are followed by the infinitive without *to*:
  - I must go now.
  - He should see a doctor.
  - You can't go home yet.
  - They couldn't open the door.

• To form questions with modal verbs, we change the order of the subject and verb. We also repeat the modal verb in short answers.

Can Should	I he they	go now?

Yes	you he they	can. should.
No		can't. shouldn't.

Some common uses of modal verbs

• Making requests:
  - Could you speak more slowly?
  - Would you open the window, please?
• Making offers:
  - Shall I open the window?
  - Can I help you?
  - I'll carry that bag for you.
  - Would you like a cup of coffee?
• Asking for and giving permission:
  - Can I come in?
  - You can sit down if you like.
  - May I use your phone?
• Giving orders and instructions:
  - You can't smoke in here.
  - You must be home by 11 o'clock.
• Giving advice:
  - You should buy a bike.
  - You shouldn't worry so much.
• Talking about ability:
  - Can you play the piano?
  - He can't swim.
• Talking about the future:
  - I'll see you on Tuesday.
  - She may/might phone this evening.
  - Don't worry. It won't hurt.

Infinitives and -ing forms

Verb + -ing

stop finish	working
enjoy like	reading the paper

• The verb *like* is usually followed by *-ing* in British English, and by *to* + infinitive in U.S. English.

Verb + to + infinitive

promise agree refuse want would like	to	help work harder speak to her

• Compare:
  - I like going to the cinema. (= I enjoy it.)
  - I'd like to go to the cinema this evening. (= I want to go.)
• *begin* and *start*
  After the verbs *begin* and *start*, we can use either *-ing* or *to* + infinitive:

They started	climbing to climb	the hill

Verb + object + to + infinitive

ask tell advise allow	them	to	see the manager leave

• *make* and *let*
  After the verbs *make* and *let*, we use the infinitive without *to*:
  - Let me help you!
  - They made me open my suitcase.
  - They didn't let anyone leave the building.

Irregular verbs

Infinitive	Simple past	Past participle
be	was/were	been
become	became	become
begin	began	begun
blow	blew	blown
break	broke	broken
bring	brought	brought
build	built	built
buy	bought	bought
can	could	(been able)
catch	caught	caught
choose	chose	chosen
come	came	come
cost	cost	cost
cut	cut	cut
do	did	done
draw	drew	drawn
dream	dreamt	dreamt
drink	drank	drunk
drive	drove	driven
eat	ate	eaten
fall	fell	fallen
feed	fed	fed
feel	felt	felt
find	found	found
fly	flew	flown
forget	forgot	forgotten
get	got	got
give	gave	given
go	went	gone (been)
have	had	had
hear	heard	heard
hide	hid	hidden
hit	hit	hit
hold	held	held
hurt	hurt	hurt
keep	kept	kept
know	knew	known
lay	laid	laid
learn	learnt	learnt
leave	left	left
lend	lent	lent
let	let	let
lie	lay	lain
lose	lost	lost
make	made	made
mean	meant	meant
meet	met	met
pay	paid	paid
put	put	put
read	read	read
ride	rode	ridden
ring	rang	rung
rise	rose	risen
run	ran	run
say	said	said
see	saw	seen
sell	sold	sold
send	sent	sent
set	set	set
shake	shook	shaken
shine	shone	shone
shoot	shot	shot

Infinitive	Simple past	Past participle
show	showed	shown
shut	shut	shut
sing	sang	sung
sit	sat	sat
sleep	slept	slept
speak	spoke	spoken
spell	spelt	spelt
spend	spent	spent
stand	stood	stood
steal	stole	stolen
swim	swam	swum
take	took	taken
teach	taught	taught
tear	tore	torn
tell	told	told
think	thought	thought
throw	threw	thrown
understand	understood	understood
wake	woke	woken
wear	wore	worn
win	won	won
write	wrote	written

Phonetic symbols

Vowels

Symbol	Example
/iː/	tree /triː/
/i/	many /ˈmeni/
/ɪ/	sit /sɪt/
/e/	bed /bed/
/æ/	back /bæk/
/ʌ/	sun /sʌn/
/ɑː/	car /kɑː/
/ɒ/	hot /hɒt/
/ɔː/	horse /hɔːs/
/ʊ/	full /fʊl/
/uː/	moon /muːn/
/ɜː/	girl /ɡɜːl/
/ə/	arrive /əˈraɪv/
	water /ˈwɔːtə/
/eɪ/	late /leɪt/
/aɪ/	time /taɪm/
/ɔɪ/	boy /bɔɪ/
/əʊ/	home /həʊm/
/aʊ/	out /aʊt/
/ɪə/	hear /hɪə/
/eə/	there /ðeə/
/ʊə/	pure /pjʊə/

Consonants

Symbol	Example
/p/	pull /pʊl/
/b/	bad /bæd/
/t/	take /teɪk/
/d/	dog /dɒg/
/k/	cat /kæt/
/g/	go /gəʊ/
/tʃ/	church /tʃɜːtʃ/
/dʒ/	age /eɪdʒ/
/f/	for /fɔː/
/v/	love /lʌv/
/θ/	thick /θɪk/
/ð/	this /ðɪs/
/s/	sit /sɪt/
/z/	zoo /zuː/
/ʃ/	shop /ʃɒp/
/ʒ/	leisure /ˈleʒə/
/h/	house /haʊs/
/m/	make /meɪk/
/n/	name /neɪm/
/ŋ/	bring /brɪŋ/
/l/	look /lʊk/
/r/	road /rəʊd/
/j/	young /jʌŋ/
/w/	wear /weə/

Stress

We show stress by a mark (ˈ) before the stressed syllable:
later /ˈleɪtə/; arrive /əˈraɪv/; information /ɪnfəˈmeɪʃn/

Acknowledgements

The authors and publishers would like to thank the following institutions and teachers for their help in testing the material and for the invaluable feedback which they provided.

ILI, Heliopolis, Egypt; The British Council, Cairo, Egypt; Lille University, Lille, France; IFG Langues, Paris, France; British Intstitute in Paris, Paris, France; IFERP, Paris, France; Beatrice Schildknecht, Wedel/Holstein, Germany; Heather Weyh, KONE, Hannover, Germany; The British Council, Athens, Greece; ELTE Radnóti Miklós Gyakorló Iskola, Budapest, Hungary; International House, Budapest, Hungary; Associazione Culturale delle Lingue Europee, Bologna, Italy; Teach In Language and Training Workshop, Rome, Italy; Cambridge Centre of English, Modena, Italy; British Institute of Florence, Florence, Italy; Toyohashi University of Technology, Toyohashi, Aichi-Ken, Japan; Cambridge School, Granollers, Spain; Senior Citizen Language and Cultural Centre, Zurich, Switzerland; Klubschule, Lichtensteig, Switzerland; Marmara Üniversitesi, Istanbul, Turkey; Yapi ve Kredi Bankasi, A.S., Istanbul, Turkey; Eyüboğlu Lisesi, Istanbul, Turkey; Ortadoğu Ingilizce Kurslari, Ankara, Turkey; London Study Centre, London, UK; Davies's School of English, London, UK; Eurocentre, Cambridge, UK; Studio School of English, Cambridge, UK; Newcastle College of Further Education, Newcastle, UK; Anglo World, Oxford, UK; International House, London, UK; Godmer House School of English, Oxford, UK; Chichester School of English, Chichester, UK.

The authors and publishers are grateful to the following copyright owners for permission to reproduce copyright material. Every endeavour has been made to contact copyright owners and apologies are expressed for any omissions.

p. 23: Adapted from a text by Iñaki Ariztimuño in *Aliens* Spring l989, City of London Polytechnic, courtesy of Heathrow Airport Ltd.   p. 30: Chart from the *New Scientist*, 25 February 1989, reprinted by permission of World Press Network Ltd.   p. 34: Texts adapted from *Book of Amazing Facts*. Text © 1988 Bamber Gascoigne. Illustrations © 1988 Joe Wright (not reprinted here). Published in the UK by Walker Books Ltd.   p. 41: Text & photograph from *The Haunted Realm* by Simon Marsden.   p. 49: 'Going for Gold' from *Me*, 19 June 1989, published by G E Magazines Ltd.   p. 56: BBC Radio 4 Logo & BBC references reproduced by permission of BBC Radio Publicity & Promotions. p. 69: Adapted article (6.9.89.) courtesy of the *Edinburgh Evening News*   pp. 74 & 75: *Board Games Round the World* by R Bell & M Cornelius, Cambridge University Press.   p. 83: Job Hunt Brochure cover reproduced by permission of the Controller of Her Majesty's Stationery Office.   pp. 87/121/122 Article adapted from 'Pilot slumped at the controls' in the *Times*, Saturday 15 July 1989, by permission of Times Newspapers Limited;   p. 92: The Dream Game adapted from the *Indy*, November 1989.   p. 101: Article adapted from *The New Internationalist*, No. 195, May 1989, by permission of New Internationalist Publications Ltd.   pp. 106 & 107: Extract from 'The Seagull' in *Plays* by Chekhov, translated by Elisaveta Fen (Penguin Classics, 1954), copyright © Elisaveta Fen, 1951, 1954; Cover of *The Penguin Book of American Verse* edited by Geoffrey Moore (Penguin Books, Revised Edition, 1983), cover copyright © Penguin Books Ltd, 1983; Poem 'This Is Just to Say' by William Carlos Williams, Collected Poems Volume I 1909–1939. Copyright 1983 by New Directions Publishing Corporation. Reprinted by permission of New Directions Publishing Corporation (U.S. & Canadian rights). Also by permission of Carcanet Press Ltd. (UK & Commonwealth rights); Extract from & cover of *One Secret Too Many* by Vanessa Grant published by Mills & Boon Ltd., reprinted by permission of Harlequin Enterprises; Extract from & cover of *The Sittaford Mystery* copyright © 1931 by Agatha Christie, by permission of Aitken & Stone Ltd & Harper Collins Publishers; 'Batman', 'The Penguin', related indicia and logos are trademarks of DC Comics Inc. All rights reserved. Used by permission.   pp. 110-111: *The Night in the Hotel* by Siegfried Lenz, *Gesamelte Erzählungen* © 1970 by Hoffmann und Campe Verlag 'Die Nacht im Hotel' Seite 164; translated by Douglas Young.   p. 115: Cartoon © Michael Heath of *The Spectator*.   p. 117: Cartoon from *The Far Side* by Gary Larson is reprinted by permission of Chronicle Features, San Francisco, CA.   p. 118: Cartoon reproduced by permission of Punch.

The authors and publishers are grateful to the following illustrators and photographic sources:

Illustrators: Julie Anderson: pp. 53, 71, 89; Nancy Anderson: pp. 21, 61, 65 *t*, 119, 120; Sarah Ball: pp. 88, 92, 97; Rowan Barnes-Murphy: pp. 19, 30 *t*, 73, 100 *b*, 113; Felicity Roma Bowers: p. 48; Paul Dickinson: p. 57; David Downton: pp. 121, 122; Carol Ann Duncombe: pp. 30, 63; Lisa Hall: pp. 10, 17, 27, 60 *t*, 68, 80–81; Lorraine Harrison: pp. 39 *t*, 52, 67, 74, 99, 114, 116, 118; Sue Hillwood-Harris: p. 24; Angela Jolliffe: pp. 13, 55; Katarzyna Klein: p. 46; Jan Lewis: pp. 15, 50, 95, 104; Maggie Ling: pp. 14, 28–29, 77, 102; Jeremy Long: pp. 26, 34; Leslie Marshall: p. 40; David McKee: p 86; Michael Ogden: pp. 18 *t*, 31, 59; Clyde Pearson: p. 65 *b*; Sue Shields: pp. 11, 91; Jane Smith: pp. 8, 62; Tess Stone: pp. 60, 75; Kaye Teale: pp. 42, 114, 116; Kathy Ward: p. 90; Annabel Wright: pp. 35, 40 *b*, 100 *t*, 115 *b*, 117 *b*; Claire Wyatt: pp. 18 *c*, 110, 111.

Photographers/Photographic sources: Ace Photo Agency: p. 98 D; Adams Picture Library: p. 66 A; Allsport/Pascal Rondeau: p. 73 E; Associated Press: p. 87 *b*; Art Directors Photo Library: pp. 17 *bl*, 66 D; 'Woman's Head with Sombrero', 1962, by Pablo Picasso. Arthothek Art Library, München. © DACS 1991: p. 108 *bl*; 'Landschaft am Meer', 1914, by August Macke. Arthothek Art Library, München. © Staatsgalerie Moderner Künst: p. 109 *t*; Aspect Picture Library: pp. 20 *tm* & *br*, 101; Barnabys Picture Library: pp. 25 *l* & *tr*, 44, 98 B, 103, 106 B; Benelux Press b.v. Holland: p. 77; John Birdsall: pp. 54 *bl*, 76 A, B, D, E, F, G & I, 112 *tl*; Luciano Boschiero: p. 16; Phil Bunce: p. 12 A; J. Allen Cash Photolibrary: pp. 17 *ml* & *r*, 28 *br*, 38 *bl*; Colorific Photo Library: pp. 20 *bl*, 22, 38 *tl*; Adrian Doff: p. 48; Greg Evans Photo Library: pp. 20 *tl*, *r* & *c*, 98 E, 106 J, 112 *tr*; Chris Fairclough Colour Library: p. 28 *tr*; Susan Ginn: p. 69 *t* & *b*; The Ronald Grant Archive: p 96 E; 'Circus Girl', by Georges Rouault. By permission of the Glasgow Museums and Art Galleries. © ADAGP, Paris & DACS, London 1991: p. 109 *bl*; Susan Griggs Agency: pp. 58 *tr*, 84 *tr*; Robert Harding Picture Library p. 106 E; Sara Hinchliffe: p. 39; Hulton-Deutsch; pp. 34, 47 *b*; The Image Bank: p. 12 I; The Kobal Collection: p 107 *bl*; Peter Lake: pp. 54 *br*, 105; Nigel Luckhurst: pp. 84 *t* & *bl*, 112 *bl*; Helen Ludbrooke: p. 12 C, D, E & F; 'Street Scene' 1935, by L. S. Lowry. "Courtesy: The Medici Society Limited", by permission of the Atkinson Art Gallery: p. 108 *t*; Movieland Wax Museum, California: p. 66 E; Jeremy Pembrey: pp. 12 *b*, 32 *tl* & *r*, 43, 47 *t*, 51, 58 *t* & *bl*, 72, 73 *b*, 82, 94, 114 *l*, 117 *l*; Photo Library International: p. 23; Picturepoint-London: pp. 17 *tl*, *mc* & *br*, 25 *br*, 28 *bl*, 38 *tr*, 54 *tr*, 64 *mc* & *mr*; Pictures Colour Library: p. 64 *ml*; Popperfoto: p. 87 *t*; The Press Association: p. 69 *r*; 'Reclining Mother and Child' by Henry Moore (1960-61, 480) © Henry Moore Foundation. Reproduced by kind permission of the Henry Moore Foundation; Lawrie Reznek: p. 56; Terry and Linda Rolfe: p. 69 *mt* & *mb*; 'Painting 1937', by Ben Nicholson. © Estate of Ben Nicholson. By permission of the Scottish National Gallery of Modern Art: p. 108 *br*; 'Icarus', 1947, by Henri Matisse. By permission of the Scottish National Gallery of Modern Art. © Succession H Matisse / DACS 1991: p. 109 *br*; Spectrum Colour Library: pp. 54 *bcl*, 64 *t* & *br*, 98 A & C; Sporting Pictures (UK) Limited: p. 73 A–D & F–H; Tony Stone Photo Library: pp. 32 *bl*, 33, 54 *tl* & *bcr*; The Telegraph Colour Library: pp. 17 *tr* & *bm*, 54 *tm*, 64 *bl*, 66 C; Tropix Photographic Library: p. 20 *mr*; Universal (United Pictures), the British Film Institute and Thames TV: p. 96 A–D; Visionbank/England Scene: p. 38 *br*; © The Walt Disney Company: p. 66 A; Zefa Picture Library/London: pp. 9, 54, 66 B, C, D & F.

t = top   *m* = middle   *b* = bottom   *r* = right   *c* = centre   *l* = left